# SEE
## *the*
# LIGHT

Inspirational Letters, Reflections, and
Life-Changing Positive Words

## Patti K. Owens

ISBN 978-1-0980-8998-6 (paperback)
ISBN 978-1-0980-8999-3 (digital)

Christian Faith Publishing, Inc.
832 Park Avenue
Meadville, PA 16335
www.christianfaithpublishing.com

Printed in the United States of America

For Dan, Chad, Shannon, Kimberly
The loves of my life.

# CONTENTS

# AUTHOR'S NOTE

I write letters. I have always written letters and many times people tell me that they saved them. They have told tell me over and over that they were the exact words that they needed to hear that day. I finally started to print and save them for myself. Many people have encouraged me to compile them and put them into a book. It seemed like an overwhelming task. However, as often happens, the Holy Spirit brought the perfect people into my life, and they made each task look simpler. Two people in particular.

The first is Mary Martin, a teacher in a class I was taking. While sharing my story of my letters, she gave me two words that completely changed my outlook: *Holy Messenger.* It gave my letter-writing a whole new level of importance. Mary became a close friend as well as a mentor and a spiritual companion. She felt strongly that my letters should find their way into a book, and she encouraged me to consider the idea. She was there at the beginning and has continued to support me in focusing on the finish line.

The second person is Sue Lamson. I was reunited with my old friend during a traumatic time in her life, and without her this book would not have one word on a page. Her encouragement and her expertise with computers was amazing, astounding, and frankly awesome. I was so overwhelmed by all the specifics, and she spent hours learning how to put my letters into this book. She was with me every step of the way. She so strongly believed in this project that when I would question or worry about the roadblocks, she would talk me out of my fears.

Both Mary and Sue could see the vision way before I could. Their determination and perseverance inspired me and filled me with much admiration and awe.

However, it was the Holy Spirit who sat on my shoulder and inspired me to write to these people who came into my life for so many different reasons. Just when I thought I didn't need to write, I would meet someone who could use a letter of encouragement. When I had no words, somehow they would appear on the page. More and more, I realized I was not the author but the typist. In obeying to sit down and write, it enhanced my life every time, and I looked forward to being part of the Holy Messenger team. These letters changed people's lives, if only for a moment or a day and often longer. Writing them has also changed my life and always for the better. Each person I write becomes important to me. I feel I am attached with a thread that can't be broken. They are forever in my thoughts, even if I never see them again.

As I was compelled to write all of these years, I am now compelled to share my letters with more than the recipients.

# PENTECOST

━━━━━━◆‹‹••›◆‹••›◆━━━━━━

I wrote this letter to a dear friend when she first learned her son had been diagnosed with bipolar disorder. It was a very scary time for her. Now several years later, she has definitely become whole, and she and her son have learned a lot on how to manage this disorder.

Well, today is my favorite feast in the church. This is the day we meet the Holy Spirit and learn that we will never be alone. He will be close enough to us to breathe his love and gifts upon us. He has shown us that he is walking with us throughout all of life's complexities. I love the flame of passion that the Holy Spirit instills in us. I don't think I could survive without that knowledge. You know when you combine knowledge with love, you are unstoppable and unbeatable. That is what you are doing right now. You are reading, you are talking to professionals, and to anyone who can help you know as much as possible about this disorder.

You are loving these people for their help in the perfect way that you do. You are sharing those qualities with your son so that he can see light. He needs the knowledge, but he also needs to feel your love.

I keep hearing this phrase over and over: "Help me to be whole." It almost makes me cry. In fact, it did, the first time I heard it. What does it mean to be whole, and what can we can do to achieve that? We are all broken people. We are flawed. Some of us are sick. Some are crippled. So how can we be whole? I know that love is a necessary component, as well as trust. Fortitude and courage are so important too. We need to experience the grace of the Holy Spirit to feel peace. Is it complicated or is it simple?

You are so special. Just remember that about yourself. You have an open heart, so half the battle is already won. I hope on this enlightened day of Pentecost that you know your worth. Depend on the Holy Spirit to lead the way and keep him close. Feel that breath of love and embrace it. The right people come into our lives right when we need them. We just have to be aware, and we will recognize them. So peace be to you and to your family. Be whole.

# PENTECOST RESPONSE

*May 22, 2018*

My friend's response below was one of the most moving responses that I ever received. This was such a huge moment in time for her, and she has never looked back. Her spiritual growth was instantaneous, and it has continued at a rate of speed that I have never before witnessed. She is truly an amazing child of God.

> *My beautiful friend, your words touch my heart and soul! I have been going to church all my life thinking and believing that I can give up control, only to jump back into the driver's seat. Today at church, I heard "Pentecost!" I felt the Holy Spirit! I felt the fire in my spirit. Yes, it brought me to tears multiple times, which happens often these days. But for the first time, I felt strong, not weak with my tears. My heart has been full of compassion and now with love for the Holy Spirit. I can become courageous, not only for myself but for my family. I feel I have been traveling this journey alone with my son. I know*

*the time he spent in the hospital saved his life, even though he is angry with me for leaving him there.*

*My prayer is that he opens his heart and mind so the Holy Spirit will guide him to accept this illness. I pray that He will give him the tools to heal and to find his peace. I pray not to get upset, to help me to slow my reaction and my response. I pray for patience. Come, Holy Spirit, watch over my family.*

# "Love Your Cancer Cells"

*I know that sounds like an oxymoron. At least that's what I thought when my friend shared those words with me while she was learning to deal with a terminal cancer diagnosis. Her doctors had given her six months to a year to live, and she had begun working with a spiritual director to guide her during this final part of her journey. One day he said to her, "Love your cancer cells because they are part of you. They are not going to go away, so don't spend what time you have left at war with your body." My friend did just that, and it changed the way she saw the world. By coming from love and not anger or fear, she focused on making a difference at least in one person's life each day. She lived for another five years and she made a huge difference in her community. She changed lives and was an inspiration wherever she went. Now, many years later, people still speak lovingly of her, remembering how she helped them in their time of need. She taught me the true meaning of love. If you love yourself just as you are, even though you aren't "perfect," you can send a lot of perfect into the world.*

—Chris A

# 1

## LOVE

*April 17, 2016*

Below is a letter I wrote to a young woman who had recently lost her in-laws. Both had suffered prolonged illnesses, and they passed away within a couple of years of each other. It was a difficult time for everyone. During hard times, you can really see someone's true colors. This woman was remarkable throughout and continues to be remarkable in so many ways today.

> We have learned valuable life lessons during your in-laws' illnesses. The most obvious one is that we certainly aren't promised tomorrow. The way we experience and handle adversity in our lives is another. The amount of grace we need just to get through the day can sometimes be remarkable. Both of your in-laws tried very hard to manifest the grace within them. They weren't always successful, but they did try. Your father-in-law had a bit of "snarkiness" in him that he tried very hard to limit, but it surfaced on occasion and often was directed at you.
>
> The beautiful part of your spirit is that you have a wonderful ability to forgive, and you were able to respond with love when he needed it most.
>
> I believe there are angels here on earth. They make the best daughters, spouses, moms, and friends, and I believe you are one of them. When I watch you interact with your loved ones and see

how you can really feel their pain and try to help in any way possible, I know you are more than a special person. You care more than most, you are aware more than most, and you love more than most. Every one thing in that sentence puts you so far above regular folks. Your capacity to love and forgive has no boundaries. I believe that one of the main reasons we are on this earth is to love one another. To love God and to love our neighbor as ourselves are the two commandments that Jesus said were the most important. Most of us have a hard time following them to the letter. We can love people if they are beautiful, or if they are kind, or if they can do something for me, but to love people without labeling them first is very difficult. I believe you have that gift. You love the downtrodden and the underdog as well as the most accomplished. I hope you realize how beautiful that is. It makes you stand out.

You are an amazing woman. You are raising your daughters with infinite love, and it shows in who they are and who they are becoming. You have created a wonderful life for your family. Continue to share the love that is so unique to you. Spread your angel wings.

*December 29, 2016*

This was a friend of mine who lost both of her parents within two months. She decided to move across the country. Selling and buying a house is always stressful, but most especially when you are still grieving.

> Well, my friend, the thought for the day is kindness. You have it in spades. I don't think you can be anything but kind to people. You know, I think in this world that seems to be filled with so much hate and violence, that there is also a lot of kindness around. If you are kind to someone, you are sending them a little bit of love, even if it is a stranger. I love that quality in you. I think you learned that from your parents and passed it on to your son. He is kind and you have to see it, experience it, to become it. You did a good job with him. You taught him to be respectful, kind, and loving. That is quite a feat.
>
> You know I only know your dad through your eyes, which means I know him through a lot of love. He provided for his family, which is what dads always are expected to do. But when it came time to really show what he was made of, he did that too. He showed so much kindness to your mom throughout her long illness. That is why the Father looked down and said I will let

her go first to give you peace of mind, and I will let you go quickly so that you don't suffer. Now, how do you fit into all of this kindness? Well, everywhere. You were there every day for him. He could talk to you about his hopes and fears and memories. He gave you a whole treasure box of beautiful memories. Why? Because you are kind and loving. You put your life on hold to be kind to your parents. No other sibling did this or even considered doing it. But as always happens, kindness is rewarded with wonderful gifts. You have him close in your heart, and he sends you a cardinal every so often to let you know he is sending his kindness and love to you.

*January 2, 2017*

This was a friend of mine who moved and she was in the middle of having a home built and living in a furnished apartment with all of her things in storage. Frustration is easy, and we have the need to make things happen more quickly.

> After getting your text this morning, I felt that you are doing fine, even though you can't always see it. You know patience comes in handy sometimes in our life and maybe this is one of those times. I know everything will work out just the way it is supposed to and that you are right where you are supposed to be. I want you to know that I am walking beside you on this journey and feel very honored to do so. These letters give me joy. We are a team, and I think a pretty brilliant one, thus the theme light.
>
> You know you have a beautiful light. Even when you aren't feeling it, it is still there for others to see. It is best when the light is there on the inside for you because when you walk your dog and remind yourself how lucky you are that you can. Some people your age and certainly my age are on walkers due to knee or hip surgery or more serious diseases. Aren't we lucky that the light is shining on us and through us for all to see? Sunrises and sunsets have their own beautiful

light, and also as we look at the ocean or at a golf course as well, I think there is always light to be found. I love the way the light in your eyes and your smile is there for all to see, so remember to pass them along for everyone you meet because it helps make their day better. Isn't it great to be kind of a beacon?

I have found that, when meeting a stranger and you share some small thing about yourself, they are so anxious to share something back. When they ask the simplest questions, try to really listen. People just need to talk sometimes. You have so much wisdom to offer. With your beautiful charism of mercy, you have that beautiful light of real caring. These little threads that you have woven in these short conversations have a way of weaving a beautiful fabric. Life and light come to mind when I think of you. Because I always think of your smile first and your giggle second. Light just doesn't get better than that.

I love that phrase in the Bible, "I am the Light of the World." So why shouldn't we try to emulate that? We could be the light on the beach, the light in the grocery store line: take your pick. You have light. Spread it around for all to uplift their day and as it always happens, it uplifts yours.

You are an amazing and wonderfully gifted person. Keep your self-assurance and if it starts to falter, sit down for ten minutes and think of all of the victories you have had in life. Think of all of the lessons that you have learned and the wisdom that has come from the failures.

You have traveled some of the roughest roads and there will be a lot of smooth sailing ahead. Listen, be watchful, be kind, and life takes care of itself.

*August 22, 2017*

This was written to a close friend of mine and I wrote this when her father passed away. I never met him, but I felt I knew him and his essence through the pure love of his daughter; I felt a part of his life. He was a writer and journaled every day of his life. She had such a beautiful read of his life. It was such a gift to give to the next generation.

First of all, my sweet, beautiful friend, I am so sorry for your loss and for that fresh hole in your heart. I know that ninety-six years was long enough to live, but particularly these last few years your Dad has played such a central role in your everyday living, that this is a loss in a very real way. I read the beautifully written obituary on the funeral home website. I know you wrote it and I couldn't help but notice how much you are your father's daughter. He was an amazing man, and I am so proud to be at the mass that will celebrate his life and his accomplishments. I know it may be too hard for you to do, but I wish that you could give the eulogy because I know that you would have the right words to describe the true essence of who he was and who he still is in the hearts of his loved ones.

I am so glad that you have had these years to really introduce him to your grandkids as well as your children. Being so far away during their childhood, they only had glimpses. I loved that he shared his life with you and that you learned new and surprising things. These were real gifts that were given and the memories will be so precious as time moves outward. I love that I got to know him a little bit through your eyes. It was always a beautiful picture. He lived a wonderful life and followed a wonderful path of spirituality and grace and faith. It doesn't get any better than that.

Being in education is such a beautiful profession. Education can truly lift one up out of tough circumstances and make available a whole new way of life. I so admire the lives he changed and helped them find a better path in life. You know, when I see you and talk to you and love you, I see those same attributes. You helped young minds love learning. You expanded their horizons. You made a difference in many lives at a point when it is so important.

I love the difference that you make in my life. I don't think there is anyone who really teaches me more than you do. After seeing you, I run home and google something that you said because you planted a seed for me to learn more. I love that about you. You are so intelligent, so bright, and so organized and competent. You take on so much with never a stumble. You don't do it for the accolades but with such humility. You love your kids and grandchildren and, most importantly, your husband with your whole heart. You help where needed, but when it gets to be too much, you have that wonderful self-awareness to say, "I am stepping back a bit."

I love the compassion that you have shown time and again in being the caregiver for your dad. That is such a big responsibility and it isn't easy. You embraced it and lovingly tended to him. He said and knew it, that it was because of you and only you that his last years were so rich. It was because of you that he was alive really. He could feel the love of your family surrounding him always. That is the beautiful picture that your dad saw when his health was failing him. He saw the real you.

You are one in a million and I mean just that. Never change because you are absolutely perfect just the way you are. You have that beautiful smile and wonderful loving personality. Keep your sense of justice and insight. Remember the real treasure that you are. I love our friendship.

*March 9, 2018*

This is a gal who was going through a very rough patch in her marriage. She was living in a lot of darkness and feeling very down about herself and her life. As happens with darkness, it finally went away, and she has much gratitude for the lessons learned and for the light that now surrounds her.

Well, love wasn't the word that I thought I was going to write about today, but there it is on the page. Your capacity to love is so great. Take a minute to sit and put your arms around yourself and hug and love yourself. Oh yes, it is worth doing. While you are doing that with a pure heart, just think of the love that you have given to the world. Your love of dogs, which is over the top, love of your grandchildren, kids, and spouses. Think of your pastor, friends, and neighbors. Beautiful, isn't it? Love makes the world go round. Feel your love going out, but now feel it flooding back from all of those people. Feel the love of God, which is even stronger. Doesn't he make you feel safe? Doesn't he make you feel calm? Doesn't he make you feel his gentleness? Love is a really good word to start and end the day.

Your job right now is to love yourself. Sleep and dream funny things, wonderful things, meaningful things. No action is required in your life right now. Feel God's love and the love of others and now love yourself and feel that too. Just sit and feel. Let those feelings rest gently on your shoulders, in your hands, and in your heart. Heal yourself through love. Take care of yourself in the quiet of your home, the quiet of a walk, the quiet of sunset. Love yourself and in that, the healing begins. Think of some of the love moments along the way.

So, my friend, you have given and received love. Love yourself. Look at who you are, accept your flaws, praise your gifts and talents, and just love you. Just know that God loves you a million times more. That is the best thought of all, isn't it?

Love is the most important part of you. Enjoy.

*July 2, 2018*

This was written to a friend who was going through a divorce after thirty years of marriage, and they reconciled. It wasn't easy, especially since her spouse was ill. She helped bring him back to health. Her spiritual life changed in a dramatic way. Through this tough time, she became the best that she could be.

> I just finished reading that book, and I hope you will enjoy reading the one I sent to you. I love that she mentions that true success in life is kindness and love. It is important to start with loving ourselves. Relaxing, reflecting, being quiet, and listening to what we hear, is an essential way to live this journey. Anyway, I think you are a true success story. You have waded through the seaweed and the strong current in the river and have found your authentic self. You see your flaws, but you see your beautiful shining spirit. I love that you walked the marathon and came out the other end stronger, better, wiser. When I look at the last couple of years in the desert and the darkness, and I see you now in the garden surrounded by light, I know how much strength you had to have to get there. Strength is something that we don't know that we possess until we need it. You

were the best person you could be in the worst of circumstances. You learned to love again and to retain your kindness. They are both so important.

*December 11, 2018*

This is a friend of mine who is on an extraordinary spiritual journey. Every time I see her, I am uplifted and inspired. I wrote this in gratitude for all that she has given me. She has this amazing energy that is bigger than life. She has this wonderful sense of humor that she brings to everything and everyone in her life. I love being part of her life whenever I am able.

> Well, my friend, you just made my day yesterday—really, my week. I am so happy for you taking this journey into Ignatian spirituality. It really is such a perfect fit for you. When we each took that first class there and you ended up in the class for spiritual director, you knew that you weren't going to do anything like that, but it was just the class that fit your schedule. When are we going to learn that we are right where we are supposed to be? Anyway, I know that to be true. You said you weren't sure what you were going to do with it, but it was so apparent to me that you are already doing it. I haven't seen you in a while, so it was so obvious to me, the change in you. You said you were tired, so you were quiet. I saw so much more than that. You had a serenity and a beautiful peaceful light surrounding you that came from your inner self. I wanted to jump across the table and see if I could touch it and steal a lit-

tle bit of it. I know it doesn't work like that. We all have to walk our path and make many really good choices for our present and our future to get there. You have been doing just that. How many times have you said yes to things totally out of your realm, from making tapes for our program, to running programs, and for helping all of the people in jail all those years you worked? You listen, you ponder, you accept. I find that so amazing.

I always think you and I have a way of looking at things the same way. But believe me, you are light-years ahead of me. If we have to come back in another life just to get it right, I hope I come back as you in that vibrant little body of yours ready to change the world. It will catapult my mind and body and soul into such a higher place. I really hope I am right about that because starting as a donkey isn't very refreshing.

Anyway, you know that I think you are amazing. I am in awe that you take these giant steps so often. So many of us have trouble just taking baby steps and believe me, they can be very trepidatious at that. Stay on your path and I know that the Holy Spirit has glorious things for you. We know at this point that age is just a number and you are the perfect example of that. I love that you help these people in their final years. You are a true blessing in so many people's lives. This new journey is already reshaping you into a new, more beautiful person!

I love you and who you are. I love your courage, your listening ear, your intelligence, your fortitude, and your willingness to be the servant to others to help them to rise and walk tall. When I think of that quote from our friend's mom, "I am awake and still here today, Lord, so what would you like me to do?" you are the most perfect example of that. I am so blessed to have you in my life. You are an inspiration to me and you, more than anyone else, show me the way.

*March 30, 2019*

This is a friend of mine who suffers from depression. She gets it every few years and has such a struggle to get well and feel good and feel normal. This one lasted much longer than usual. She was in this darkness for nine months. It is always scary because she doesn't know if this will be her new normal.

> Well, my dear friend, here I am walking through this with you once again. So, on this gloomy, cloudy day, I always know that the sun is behind those clouds, and it is just a matter of time before they move over and out and the sun comes through again. This is what I believe with this rather long bout with depression. Spring is coming, and I believe it is going to bring that spring into your step and focus back to your consciousness. The Holy Spirit is going to put the right people in your life with the right combination of medication and good weather, and you will be in the light once again.
>
> I am sure that when you are around that beautiful baby and her parents, light shines through her to you. She loves you just like the rest of the world. I could see the joy in both of your expressions in that picture. Even with no makeup on, there is pure emotion of love and joy from both of you. I am so happy that you can

see them regularly, even if it isn't often. FaceTime is a blessing as well, with the videos they send. I love this modern technology when it comes to grandchildren because you get to see all of the first times: crawling, walking, and first words. Just talking about or thinking about that beautiful little girl brings a little of that light back into your eyes. I think that bright-eyed baby might be a little bit of the solution. She can't figure out the meds, or have the ear of the psychologist, or nutritionist, or friends, but she has your heart, and that is part of the cure.

During Lent, I have written a short story every day of someone I meet or see looking for three things: surprised, moved, inspired. You are my person for today. You surprise me always with just your presence; it is always amazing. You move me with your fortitude to keep on going in the darkest of times. You inspire me with your capacity to love. So thank you for being one of my amazing Lenten people. You and they make my days better, and hopefully me better as well.

Know that this cloud will be lifted and light and sunshine will be in your life again. This is not your life in the future.

*April 11, 2019*

This is a friend of mine who was suffering from depression. She was living in darkness that had lasted six months when I wrote this letter and she was concerned that it would last forever. It took nine months, but in a day it all changed and the depression was gone.

> After this weekend with your granddaughter, I am sure your heart was filled with love. You don't have to try to fake it; it is just there. I think that God was there and the Holy Spirit had you all in His loving arms.
>
> This week, I read an article that we were created in the image and likeness of God. Can't you remember memorizing those words from our catechism when we were kids? I never really tried to define what they meant. I just wanted to pass the test. This person was saying that it is all about love, how much God loves us and how much we love him back, when we are going through tough times. I think we forget how much we love God and how much we need him in our daily conversation.
>
> It reminds me of the wedding song with the line "Where there is love there is life." Isn't that the truth? I love to have love in my heart every morning because the sun shines brighter and even the clouds are less gray. That is my wish for

you. Start your day with a sentence I love—make it something small or big or the same thing every day. Just try to remember how important it is to love and that having love in your heart is such a gift. I love you through your pain and heartache. More importantly, so does the Holy Spirit. He will help to bring you out of this darkness. He gave you those moments of joy with your little one so you don't forget they are out there.

You are such a quality person. You are surrounded by people who love you, from friends to family. God loves you. I hope that at least you can start to love yourself. Ask the Holy Spirit to help you see the love in the people and things around you. Try to see the beauty of creation. Love is what makes the world go round. I hope you can recognize some love out there today.

*November 24, 2019*

I met this gal and her girlfriend at a seminar and we decided to meet for lunch. We spent this wonderful afternoon together. As we talked and she discussed how many things she did for so many people, I was blown away. There just weren't that many hours in a day. She had a very stressful job, but she found time to be of service to others.

It was such a beautiful day yesterday, spending some of it with you. I loved hearing your story. But one of the most beautiful phrases of the day was from your friend with her wonderful short-hand of explaining things: "You play tennis with your heart." That visual that I got keeps changing in my mind, and every time it gives me a warm and wonderful feeling. That just makes me know that kindness runs completely through you. It is a critical part of your DNA. People can be kind and I love that, but I think that you are kindness, and that is different. Who hops on a plane every six weeks and flies halfway across the country after working all week to spend a weekend with their family? You know the importance of family and you keep them close, even with the distance. That is love and kindness.

I love people like you who take the time to plant the bulbs. After a long winter, I love when I am taking a walk and all of a sudden I see the daffodils or tulips peeking through, and I know we are coming into spring. You make all of these meals for shelters. You are in charge of cooking for church suppers and also cook for your family You take the time to nourish people, and once again showing love and kindness and service.

Singing in the choir and sharing your beautiful voice with the congregation is wonderful. I have a friend who was from Korea and she has a beautiful voice. When my sister was ill, she would come to her house and sing her hymns in English and then in Korean. It was such a comfort to my sister. Then she started volunteering at the hospital. She would take her music hymnal and do the same thing. She would ask them their favorite hymn and sing in both languages. She couldn't wait for those days and the patients were enriched in a very special way. I loved the way she used her gift. That might not be your fit, but if you have an open heart and an open mind, the Holy Spirit will show you the way that will give you the most joy.

All of these gifts, you send out to the world. I am not sure if you realize all of the joy that you create, but I hope you feel the joy come back to you. I hope you know your worth and how you brighten the day for those around you.

You are unique in your gifts, and you are making so many people's lives better with your service and your kindness and your love. I still love "playing tennis with your heart."

*May 11, 2020*

This was written to a friend of mine who lost her husband to the coronavirus. I had been journeying with her through letters during his illness and ultimately his death. It was a devastating time. He was healthy and traveling on vacation one minute and gone a month later. She had tested positive, so she was quarantined for five weeks. To have all of this going on and not being able to hug and hold anyone or see anyone face to face was that much harder. This letter was written in the weeks after he had passed away.

Sometimes receiving is what it is all about. You are in the situation to just receive. In the last few weeks, how many kindnesses have been sent your way in food, flowers, cards? No one expects anything back, but they just want you to receive their love and caring. They want you to know how important you are in their lives. There will be a time when all that receiving turns back around into giving, but not now. Now you are the focal point. Now the Holy Spirit is looking upon you with a special love to see you through. Just receive. Hopefully this week you will receive the news that you can leave your house. Just as the weather starts to turn warmer and the leaves will be in full bloom, you can receive the beauty of spring and breathe in the smell of spring. Receive the blessings. Receive the sadness and grief.

Know that it won't last forever. There is beauty in the world and in your life and, little by little, you will be able to receive that too. I hope you will be able to receive the hugs of your little ones in the near future that will bring such warmth.

This part of this journey is nearing the end. I know there will still be challenges, but I hope you can see and receive the goodness that comes your way too.

# PARK THE CAR

*This is a story that a friend of mine shared with me many years ago, and it is relevant today as well. I say these words many times, and they always work.*

*When she was twenty years old, she and a girlfriend decided to drive out west to see the Grand Canyon. After many days of travel, they got to their destination, but they couldn't find it. They drove back and forth along this highway and finally stopped a stranger and asked if he could give them directions. He said, "Park the car," so they did and followed him for fifty yards across the highway, and they were looking at the most beautiful vista of the Grand Canyon.*

*So when things are hectic, and I feel like I am running in circles, I stop and say to myself, "Just park the car," and in moments I am relaxed and can see things more clearly. The beautiful vistas are right there and after my amazement and awe, these are always followed with gratitude for the many blessings in my life. Those words of wisdom have come to my rescue many times over the years.*

—Cindy K

# 2

# GRATITUDE

*January 22, 2017*

This was written to a friend who was second-guessing some decisions she had made. She seemed to be dwelling on the negative things that were happening and ignoring the good things.

> We are having a pretty cloudy and windy day here with maybe some severe weather coming in later. When I look outside, I can see a few rays of sunshine coming through the clouds. It makes me realize that the sun hasn't gone anywhere; it has just been hiding for a bit. The good stuff is always there, but sometimes it is hidden by the bad stuff, and we have to look a little harder to find it.
>
> What do our eyes see and our ears hear? When I'm feeling grateful, the sunshine just seems a little brighter. Life is full of choices, so why not try to make the most positive ones each day? Not every day is perfect, but if you look really hard, you will learn to recognize the goodness that is always there. With a heart filled with gratitude, every day seems better.

*March 4, 2018*

This is a friend who was going through a divorce after a very long marriage. It was very complicated. In the end, they did not divorce. It brought some challenges, but they worked through them and many things did get better.

> Okay, so I woke up this morning and I realized we can always be grateful for something—sunrises and sunsets, friends, daughters, grandchildren, life, health, and not the least, faith. We can be grateful for the future. Your life will change and, I believe, in very good ways. We can't see what it is, but I know it will be of your own making. There may be a companion out there to share it. Who knows what will happen, but you are in God's hands, and I know that is the best place to be.
>
> Gratitude can help to look forward to a brighter future and get out from under the cloud. One thing I know for sure is when the clouds go away, there is full sunshine. So just take a minute and fantasize and dream of the best, right future you can have. Make up whatever you want; it is your dream. Stay there a minute to relish it. Know in your heart that is where you are headed, and that is where your journey is taking you. Be

grateful that you can dream and that you can smile when you are doing it.

Be grateful for the knowledge this part of your journey has given you. Be grateful to know the strength that you have found in that small body of yours. Be grateful for the little things that are happening and for the bigger things down the road. Be grateful for the God that lives in your heart, he is getting you through this. I just know there is a whole new beautiful life ready to reveal itself. I am grateful for that and hope you are too.

*April 20, 2018*

My friend had just received the news that her son was bipolar. He was in bad shape and she knew it was the beginning of a very long journey. In fact, they are still on this journey. They have made progress and have slid backward a bit, but with each step, they are growing in wisdom. Time will tell where their journey will take them and how it will all work out.

> *Gratitude,* that seems to be the word for the day. I was going to start this letter by saying that, even in darkness, there is always something to be grateful for. Then I got your text. Wow, look at that sliver of light coming through.
>
> I think if you can start the day with gratitude for one or two things, it changes the way the day plays out. For me, it can be as simple as noticing the beautiful blue sky with no wind, when I can walk in peace, listening to the birds and seeing the trees beginning to bud. Time melts away for me on my walks, and in no time an hour has passed, and I am amazed to be home.
>
> I was thinking if your son could experience a little light, like the sliver of a new moon; he would want to do everything or anything to see a full moon. Drugs and alcohol aren't the answer, and hopefully he will learn that fact. Be grateful for his psychologist, the first cog in this wheel,

and understand that this journey will involve one step at a time. Thankfully, baby steps count. Since I have never been a giant stepper, I know this to be true. It might take longer, but he will get there.

Take a break and do something that is just pure fun for you. Go for a walk in the woods, go window-shopping, go to a coffee shop, and people watch and make up a scenario about what they are doing. If you think it might be helpful, write a few lines in a journal. Make them about you only. How has your injury affected the way you look at life—good, bad, and in what way?

I know if you could, you would fix this, because you are the fixer, but this is one time you have to sit on the sidelines. Use your thoughts to send your love and hopefully he will get it. Be grateful that there are people whom you can turn to for help.

It is with gratitude that he is in a situation where there are no outside stimuli. I hope he can stay there long enough to heal and feel the light. I wish the same for you. Relax and enjoy the sliver of light and crave the full moon. All that is required is love from afar. Fill your heart with it and squeeze out the darkness. Bring your beautiful kindness to everyone you meet. Rejoice that you are whole.

I am grateful that we have reconnected. We have walked more than one dark alley together, but we survived and we are loved. You are a special kind of person who has helped so many along the way. Accept the kindnesses that you find in the most unusual places. Watch for them and smile when you experience them. Be grateful for the smallest of things. Spoil yourself today by noticing all the good things that there are in your life. Today is all about you. It has a great ring to it, doesn't it? What a proclamation! Alleluia.

*April 30, 2018*

I wrote this letter to my very good friend's daughter. She had just stated chemotherapy following her surgery for breast cancer. She was always a very loving person and, as often happens, all that love from family and friends comes back to you when you need it most. Her older son lived on the opposite coast, and her mother lived even further away. But everyone was there for her. Now a few years later, she is doing well and enjoying her wonderful life.

> Gratitude seems like an odd word to use when you have cancer and are in the middle of treatments that make you sick. Where is there room for gratitude? I guess these are the moments in life that show us who we are and what we are made of. They often change the path we have been following—usually for the better. For one thing, I am sure you have found strength that you didn't know you had. I bet you realize gratitude when you look at your husband who is by your side for every step on this journey. Or when your son, who is so comforting, calls you often just to talk and support you. You two have such a special bond. Your mom too is always there for you as is your beautiful daughter. At her young age, she is probably frightened, but I am sure she is her caring for you in her own loving way.

So I think there is always room for gratitude, even in the most difficult of times. When you finish chemo, you will have turned one corner and will be well on your way to being fully healed. And even though you face more treatments and surgery in the future, you will make it to the end. And I will be grateful for your full recovery.

I am grateful to the doctors who have figured things out, although I wish the path had been easier and quicker. I am also thankful for the kindnesses shown by the medical staff that you have met. I will bet that there is one person who stood out in the crowd. She or he has that true gift of healing.

I am grateful that your body, mind, and soul are healing in a very unique way. And I am grateful that you are one of my best friend's two perfect daughters.

Have a beautiful day, one filled with the warmth of the sun and of love.

*September 18, 2018*

This young man was at a crossroads in his life as he began his journey down the very rough road of self-awareness. He quickly learned that two steps forward can sometimes become one step back, but he kept trying and that is the important thing. This is just one of many letters I wrote to my bipolar friend.

> I want to share a story of mine with you. I have decided to write a book. As I think about it, I know what I want the content to be, but truthfully I have no idea how to get a book published. Then, while I was walking this morning, I realized I don't have to see the whole journey. I just have to do what I can today. I trust that I will meet the right people who will support me and lead me where I need to go. Maybe it won't be a book or maybe it will be. I just know what I am going to do today.
>
> That got me thinking about you. As you know, I have been praying for you for the last six months, and in that time you have come a long way. You keep putting one foot in front of the other, and I'm sure it isn't always easy. You are fortunate to have family and friends who really care about you and support you in every way they can. You have medication that helps you stay on track. You have a psychologist who

is teaching you how to travel this new path, and you are learning to trust and to share. I promise you that the baby steps you are taking now will get bigger, and they will become more frequent.

Now, my last suggestion in this very long letter is to exercise. I think it is so important to clear your mind, to relax your body. Do what works for you. I walk and love the way I feel at the end. So walk, jog, work out with weights or weight machines. Do whatever works for you, but exercise.

I think you are amazing in all you are accomplishing.

*June 25, 2019*

A friend of mine was going through a divorce. She was also having health problems and was trying to sell her house and buy a new one. She had a huge list of things to do and being in pain made it more difficult to get anything done. Thankfully, she had amazing fortitude and she managed to get through all of it in good shape.

Gratitude might be the last thing you're experiencing today, but I think we should practice being grateful at all times. When we're grateful for even the smallest things, like a summer breeze, a day filled with sunshine, or a hug from a child, these change the way we look at life. It makes us look for the good wherever we are.

I can't begin to imagine the pain you've been through with this kidney stone, but I have a feeling you have met some remarkable people who have helped you along the way. God doesn't send us into the darkness without adding a few sparklers and fireworks to light our way. I believe if we can be grateful for the smallest blessings during the worst of times, then the rest falls into place.

I hope we can get together this week. I have really missed our time together. Know that you are in my thoughts, and I pray for your health and welfare. I look forward to hearing what's been going on with you, and I want you to know I am not here to judge, only to listen. We are walking together while you are making some difficult decisions. In the end, things will be what they're meant to be.

Take care of yourself so you can be healthy and can be there for your family. God be with you. Take advantage of the grace that he is freely giving you every day.

*July 4, 2019*

I wrote this letter to a friend who was going through a divorce. Even though she was the one who had asked for the divorce, she didn't realize how there would be so many real challenges and bumpy roads. Second-guessing yourself can be stressful, and starting a new life means leaving the old behind. The path ahead isn't always clear.

> Grief is a funny thing; it shows up when we least expect it. Healing from grief is the same way. One morning you wake up and although the loss is still there, you can feel surrounded by joy. If you are grieving from the death of a loved one, you can take comfort in knowing that person is in a better place. If it is a friendship you have lost, you may have found another that is even more enriching. And if you're working through a divorce, you can find your new meaning in the life you create for yourself. In all the losses, if we are thoughtful and we are wise, our love and friendship with God will become more meaningful and profound. In my experience, the discord of our lives can bring about so many wonderful things if we live each day with gratitude. It's like the sun is always there, but it is hidden from us at times by a cloud. God is constantly showing us that there is much joy in the world, but we often need to walk through a wall of grief to find it.

Then, not only will you feel it, but you will relish in it. His love for us is always there, but there are moments when we doubt it or we don't feel it. If we are willing to learn the lessons and to grow in goodness, we will feel the warmth again with much more fervency.

I think you possess a lot of wisdom. You don't snap back in anger, and you keep your children above the fray. This divorce creates a lot of change in their lives, but you are making it as smooth as possible. Your wisdom has made this plan a doable thing, but be open to changes along the way. Often plan A is changed to plan B, C, or D. They all work to make a whole. Know that you have only today to worry about. Make a small list each day of things you want to get done or phone calls you need to make. If you don't get them done, they go to the top of tomorrow's list. If it takes three days, then so be it. Know that the Holy Spirit is literally holding your hand and he won't let you get lost on this path.

I am so inspired by you. There are so many things on your plate right now, and when all of this is over, your life will seem like a walk in the park. You will still have problems to solve, places to be, friendships to attend, and most importantly, children to raise, but hopefully for most of the time, it will be one crisis at a time. I am sorry for the sadness and the loss that you are feeling, but I know in my heart that beyond this, you will have a life that is filled with happiness, joy, and best of all, peace. Your faith and trust in God will get you right where you need to be. You have the strength, the wisdom, the fortitude, and the courage to make this happen. Joy, love, and peace are just around the corner. I feel everything begins with gratitude. Be grateful today for the smallest things, for the sunshine, for the joy a new day brings, and for the gift of your wonderful children. The rest will fall into place.

# Baby Steps Count

*I am not sure where I first heard this, but I have adopted it as my mantra. I have taken so many baby steps in my life. You might say I am a slow learner and certainly not a giant stepper most of the time, but when I learned that baby steps count, it changed my way of looking at things. Like they say, life isn't a sprint; it is a marathon and if all you do is take baby steps, you are moving forward, not standing still. So give yourself a break and know that whatever you are doing, even if it is a small thing, baby steps count. You will get where you are supposed to be. That is what really counts. I have a friend who was going through a very tough time, and I wrote her a letter. She wrote a response and she told me her friends had been telling her to just take baby steps. I couldn't help but share my mantra with her. She wrote back that she was going to add, COUNT, to the phrase, with it all in capital letters. It somehow changes the importance of baby steps, I think.*

—Patti O

# 3

# JOY

*April 4, 2015*

I wrote this letter to a young man who worked in a big box store. Whenever I saw him, he was not only pleasant, but also helpful. He always made me feel better. I didn't know his name at the time, but I wrote him this letter and delivered it when I saw him. He showed it to his boss and ended up getting a promotion. We have kept in touch since. The last time I saw him, he and his partner had married.

> I wanted to write you a note and tell you how much I have had the privilege to know you over the years of shopping in your store. I have often told you that you are the best at what you do. I still think you could run the store, but I understand your misgivings about job security. You are so bright. I think you would be great at many things.
>
> First of all, I want to mention your sense of style. It is exquisite. You wear so much jewelry but I can't think of one piece that you should eliminate. It all works. I have a feeling that the artistic part of you goes beyond just the clothes. I imagine where you live exudes peace and tranquility with a punch of color, style, and wonderful good taste.
>
> I know that working with the public can be challenging. People bring their baggage and fling it at the first person they see. Being outwardly

gay and proud of it, I only hope that you don't get too much mean spiritedness. I wish for you a wonderful partner to share your life because I think love is the most important of our feelings. It is important to have faith, hope, and charity but to me, you have all of those if you have love. I can feel your love for others when you talk. You have shared your gratitude for the blessings in your life. I think we can't truly start our day without gratitude in our hearts.

I just want you to know that you stand out above the others in the store and that you are an inspiration to me and to others. I love that you know who you are and share it with us, the customers. I will understand if you go on to bigger things, but I want you to know that if you do, you will be missed. When I come into the store, I always look around to see if you are there and am disappointed if you aren't.

Know that you make a difference in people's lives in a very good way. Have a wonderful day. God looks down and smiles on your spirit and he is pleased.

*December 22, 2016*

This was a friend who was suffering from depression. I wrote her a note every day for a month. She was finally starting to come out of it, and I just wanted to remind her what joy felt like since depression kills the joy and love in your life. Although she has beaten two more bouts with this awful disease, there is always that possibility that it could return at any time and that she won't come out of it again. She is a truly an amazing and strong person.

> Joy is such an important emotion, and even if you can't feel it right now, I just want to remind you that it is out there. Sometimes it is great to just have a really good belly laugh—a laugh-until-you-cry laugh. Try turning your favorite comedian on the computer and just relax and laugh and feel the joy go through your body. We laughed like that at a year old and at ten years old, so why not laugh like that at this age? It might take some practice, but it could be worth the effort.
>
> Think of all of the joy that you can remember from your lifetime that is spread so magically around this season. Bring those memories to the foreground to relive the joy.
>
> I love you in joy or in sadness, love you thinner or thicker, I love your soul, your beautiful face, and your wonderful, dark, curly hair.

You always give me joy, and I want to offer it back to you.

You are making your life work against all odds, so I know when you work this hard, you will beat this. You will get your life back and you will see the light at the end of this tunnel.

*December 23, 2016*

This is a friend of mine who was going through a depression, and I wrote her to cheer her up. She was getting much better, and I didn't want her to be upset because she hadn't done much for anyone in a few months. I learned so much about depression from her. A person really loses oneself. They forget the good things about themselves and can only see the negative.

> When I think of you, the words that always come to mind are *joy* and *sweetness*. With your sweetness, you are always spreading joy. How many times in your life has someone told you how sweet you are, or thanked you because that was such a sweet thing to do? I would bet a lot. Like I say to my grandchildren, "How high can you count?" This loving, caring, giving, and spreading joy is just something that you do without thinking. How many blueberry pies, cookies, and cupcakes have you made and delivered to people to make their day better? All of that takes time, but they are filled with your love, which makes them taste even better.
>
> Next I would say the sweet words that you say to people to help them in tough moments, or joyful moments, or just chatting, spread joy and help to bring smiles to everyone. You take the time to visit someone who is ill instead of just

staying home and saying a quick prayer. You are a doer and you don't let any stone go unturned. Thank you for all of your sweetness because we all learn to be a better person from you.

*February 5, 2017*

This gal was a single mom whose son had graduated from college and started his career. She decided to sell her home and move halfway across the country to start a new life. It took a lot of courage.

> I was thinking this morning about perception. I know that God loves us unconditionally, as do many people. I wonder why we can't always see it and feel it. If we could, it would make our decisions have so much more clarity and conciseness. Our perception of ourselves—especially women, I think—look at the negative and dwell on what we can't do rather than what we can. If we meet someone who has that great confidence in herself, we aren't sure she is correct. The perception of others and of the world has to start with ourselves. Do we see ourselves for real? Do we see our talents, skills, and gifts? Then we need to not only see it but feel it and believe it.
>
> That is why I am so in awe of you right now. You have taken the first steps to build a life that totally fits you and who you truly are today. I don't want you to shortchange yourself. I hope that your perception of the beautiful, colorful ocean sunrises helps you feel the infinite possibilities that are available in this new chapter. I envision you organizing your new place and making

it a thing of beauty, peace, and hospitality. Life has so many twists and turns, but there is joy and laughter along the way.

I always come back to the same phrase when I think of you: "You are amazing." Your quick and honest intuition is perfect. Your assessment of others is great and often entertaining because of your wonderful sense of humor. So we come to your perception of yourself, which always seems to have a tougher set of rules and regulations. Let it give you comfort that your choices are the correct ones, the smart ones, and the best ones. Know that each step is on a path that is your purpose.

*May 25, 2019*

This is a friend who has changed her life in almost every way, and she is still trying to finish the picture, but she continues to find her way in the most unique ways. That experience was almost mystical for me, and I wasn't surprised that her face was in the middle of it. She is an extraordinary person, and I love watching her journey.

> I was walking this morning and your name and your face came into my mind, and I couldn't help but feel joy. It is such a great way to start my day. I hope all is well with you. I hope, as well, that this spring and Easter season is joyous for you. I can't think of anyone whom I would like to send a pile of joy more than you. So I am doing just that, and it is yours for the taking.
>
> When I was walking today and praying a bit, asking for grace to live my best life, I came upon two cardinals just standing in the street— one was a girl and the other a boy. They didn't seem to mind that I was walking toward them. The girl would hop/fly a couple of feet and then the boy would follow suit. They did this several times and then they landed on a rock. I stopped to watch, smile, and feel the love. Finally, they flew into a shrub and I couldn't see them. It was magical for me. That is when you came into my mind. Anytime I see a cardinal when I am walk-

ing, I always feel it is a good omen. So I couldn't help but wonder what this dance meant. Why didn't they leave as I walked closer? I don't know the answer, but I feel blessings coming your way. Be watchful and aware. There is an awakening. Will a cardinal pass your path?

I look forward to seeing you soon.

*January 6, 2020*

I met this wonderful woman on our many trips to Florida. She always makes me feel better than I did before I talked to her. She is very special. After I wrote this letter, I heard that she goes to an elementary school and helps with the young children. I am sure they look forward to the days when she comes to help because she brings joy, and I'm sure she makes them feel better about themselves in every way.

> Joy and giving. Your letter sweater video doing the splits made me laugh. You always give me joy in big packages. You always make me smile and even laugh, but I am always awed by your generosity of spirit. I love to watch you spread the fairy dust everywhere. We are all—and I mean the world—better off that you are in it.
>
> You are so giving and so generous and so thoughtful. There is constantly someone—many times your grandchildren (how lucky are they to have their Gigi), and others' grandchildren—thanking you. You remember birthdays and every event in peoples' lives. I just love that generous and loving spirit. We are all given gifts that we give back to the world. I always am honored to meet someone who has the extraordinary gift of giving because it is always succeeded by real joy to the receiver. You are surrounded by joy and, believe me, people try to get in that little circle.

Now, let's talk sense of humor and light in the room. You are downright funny. There is always wonderful laughter around you. You end up being the most popular kid on the block. When I sit back and observe, you are always so interested in the other person's story. They have your complete attention.

There are not very many people who are the light in the room; otherwise, we would all be blinded. I have watched the ones in our large Irish family, so I consider myself an authority. Continue to spread that light and joy wherever you go. The great thing about using your gifts is that the love and joy always circles back around and comes back to you. One last thing, I love your curly hair. It looks good wet, dry, and in between. I find you amazing with that wonderful quality of kindness. Be true to you, and then life will seem to take care of itself.

# COME HOLY SPIRIT

*I was reading one day and I saw those words: "Come Holy Spirit." I tend to take short cuts when I can. I sometimes don't want to pray, and I meet people who are having difficulties and they don't want to pray. They might be angry or sad with the world and their life at that moment. At those times, I suggest to myself and others to just take a moment and say three words: "Come Holy Spirit." It takes literally a few seconds. What have we got to lose, right? Well, I look outside afterward or go for a walk and the sun is brighter and the trees are many shades of green and the birds are singing and all seems right with the world. It never fails to make a difference, so my thought is if you don't ask, you might never experience it. It is the shortest prayer I know, but when I ask him to come, he always shows up.*

*Come, Holy Spirit, I love it.*

—Patti O

# 4

## GRACE

*February 13, 2015*

A friend of mine had been through a lot and her marriage was ending. I wrote this letter to her at the beginning of her divorce. Now, five years later, she is helping others find their way. She is a major inspiration to me, and I am grateful every day for her friendship.

> These were the words I woke up with this morning when I thought of you. Since you are my teacher, my mentor, and thankfully my friend, I am writing you another letter. Although it may not be my place, I know that the spirit works through me. I am just the typist.
>
> I know there are many changes going on in your life. I know that selling your house and moving to a condo community was a huge step, but one I feel so very strongly was the right step. It is totally your place, and you are free to make all new memories and to start a fabulous new life there. I can't help but see beautiful fireworks with beautiful sunrises and sunsets in your future. Your aura is brighter than it has ever been, even with the burdens that you are carrying.
>
> In the car today, I was listening to the radio and thinking and praying for you and the speaker kept repeating one phrase over and over: "Remember that you have God's favor." I think that is so true. I am sure you are going to appre-

ciate your new home and will love the life you are creating. I wish I could give you specifics, but I know for sure it is beyond your dreams. God has amazing things in store for you. He spoke loudly to you when you were cut off at your knees so that you knew he was present. Now, he is whispering to you every day and giving you direction. You know how to listen, to ask, to communicate, and to act. What more can God want from any of us? You spread love wherever you go. Those two most important commandments—love God and love your neighbor—is exactly how you live. Continue on your journey with no fear.

*February 15, 2018*

I had a conversation with a woman in a grocery store recently and it touched my heart. For some reason, I felt compelled to write the following letter to the young woman we talked about, and I delivered it to the restaurant where she worked. I spoke to her for a second. I never saw her again and never heard from her, but she had taught me a lesson about quick judgements. I will always be grateful.

> I don't know you, but I wanted to write you a letter because of a conversation I had with a woman at the grocery store. She mentioned that she had arranged a celebration at your restaurant for her father's eighty-eighth birthday. When you approached, her first thought was *Purple hair, this is going to be a long day.* How often do we make those quick judgements that have nothing to do with the actual person? It turned out that you were the best waitress she had ever had. You got everyone's orders correct, even the one niece who had very specific requests. You did an amazing job, and you did it with grace and ease.
>
> Now, I have never eaten at your restaurant, but it has perked my curiosity, and I find I want to go there and meet the beautiful purple-haired young lady. I don't know what else you are doing with your life, but I truly hope you are following your passion. My guess is that you are intelligent

and have an amazing memory, great organizational skills, and also a bit of charisma. I am sure there is much more to you than that, but those gifts can take you a long way.

Thank you for proving to us that purple hair is just a personal choice, and it doesn't tell us anything about the heart and spirit of the person. Judgments are so easy to make, but all of us have a story that is so much more interesting than our outward appearances. I wish you well on your journey of life.

*January 24, 2017*

I wrote this letter to my friend who had moved across the country and was building a house. It was a stressful time for her. There were mountains she traversed and she made them into molehills. She showed so much strength and fortitude. I journeyed with her for a few months, and we have written often since and she is doing well.

> Sit and contemplate your strengths. I see you as strong and accomplished. Do you? I think if you look at your whole life, you will see how much strength you have had to make a beautiful and fulfilling life. Look at the last year and a half. Look at it realistically, not in what you didn't do but what you did do. Think of the strength it took some days to just survive and breathe.
>
> You did it with grace and strength and courage and love. Look in the mirror and tell that person how much you love her and that you see the amazing strength she brings to the table. I read this phrase today that I love: "Take my hand in joyful trust, letting me guide you and strengthen you." Doesn't that just sound breezy? Joyful trust, I really like that thought. Strength is one of those attributes that God gives us when we ask for his guidance and help. When brought to our knees, we realize we can't get up without help, but with help, we find our inner strengths.

Relax into your strength, depend on it, and nurture it. Adding joyful trust to the equation makes strength stronger and more flexible.

Have a beautiful day, one filled with grace. You bring grace to every situation, so share it along with your wonderful strength. Your house builders will benefit from it as well.

*September 6, 2017*

This friend of mine has many gifts and talents. She is a leader and she has a very close relationship with her God. She helps people in many ways, and she always says yes when he asks her for her services. I am grateful for her inspiring words, for the visual symbols she gives me, so I can not only see the meaning, but I can feel it.

> Somehow I am being inspired to take a journey with you. I have many words buzzing in my brain, but the most important one is inspiration. It is about you being inspired and then really inspiring others. I see you always in front of a crowd, giving people food for thought. They leave walking away just a bit above the ground. They have smiles on their faces, and their thoughts are pumping in their brain as well as in their heart. Not everyone has the ability to inspire. I believe that is saved for a chosen few.
>
> It is quite a responsibility to help people better themselves in whatever way possible. You help us find our "authentic selves." I think that really means that we discover the path that helps us to get to salvation.
>
> So continue to feel and spread the inspiration, doing this as a spiritual companion or if you are speaking to a group. Each time you share your inspiring message, you send someone

out with love in their heart and then they impact someone else. I love the domino effect of love shared. Continue to listen to your God and then to inspire.

Thank you for uplifting my spirit whenever you speak to me. And thank you on behalf of all the others whom you have inspired. I know there are many. Your gift is special, and I love that you are using it.

*February 15, 2018*

My friend was going through a challenging time in her life. Her husband was chronically ill and everything, including caregiving, was falling on her shoulders. There is little time to figure things out.

Sometimes I have trouble sleeping. It is okay because I wake up fine and figure I really didn't need the sleep. When that happens, I often dream or see things more clearly, and those images stay with me. Last night I was thinking of you, and it was all about light. Have you ever been to a concert and at the end people turn on their lighters to show their appreciation to the performer. It starts with just one light and then it multiplies. When you are on the stage looking out, it is truly a magical sight. You can't see individual faces, but the sea of lights is there. I couldn't help but think that this is what is happening to you. You are in this darkness, but hopefully you will see that first light and then it will multiply.

You are filled with this beautiful grace and you are surrounded by a wonderful aura wherever you go. One by one, angels greet you with their light.

I love that you took that small step, which ended up being a pretty giant step, on this journey. You protected yourself and your livelihood. You are working so hard to take care of your husband, to cook, clean, and to shop. You took action and everyone you meet is there to shine their light on you. The darkness inside your house leads to love and lightness when you walk outside.

I admire your willingness to be vulnerable by sharing your story with others. When you do that, people want to help you. Look at the journey you have been on the last year or two. Look where you started and look where you are now. You know who you are; I hope you realize what a wonderful person that is.

Continue to shine your light on the world and continue to look for the light all around you. God has not abandoned you. Trust that he has this figured out. He is the light of the world. Stay living in the light. People are good, and life is good. You are smart and you are strong, but remember to lean on others. They will be there for you and you will be fine. I admire you so much.

*March 11, 2018*

A friend of mine was considering a divorce after thirty years of marriage. She and her husband stayed together, but they hadn't made that decision when I wrote this letter. I could almost see the physical grace that she received each day. She accepted it and used it in the best possible way. Her life wasn't perfect, but she was able to feel grateful for all the good things in her life.

> *Grace* happens to be my favorite word. I recently found out that the Greek word for spiritual gifts, *charisma*, comes from *charis,* the root word for grace. I love the realization that our gifts are our grace. Take those many graces that have been bestowed on you and spread your gifts around. The Holy Spirit has surrounded you with a circle of grace. Live in that circle of grace right now.
>
> I love to see how grace manifests itself in others. Yours starts with compassion, which leads to love. Your compassion allows you to see the grace in others. It enables you to help them grow.
>
> I believe grace is the positive air that makes the world go round. If you could see the view of the world from above, the light you see is the grace in people. Treasure your grace and treasure your gifts. You have taught me so much with your ability to see the grace in others.

*December 19, 2018*

I wrote this to a young man who, at twenty, was diagnosed with bipolar syndrome. He was trying to adjust to his new life. This is one of many letters that I have sent to him.

> You have been on my mind lately and you are always in my prayers. Many times, when I think of you, the words *strength* comes up. When I hear one of your stories, I am amazed at the amount of strength it takes you to get through a day. When you were a lot younger, you had that inner strength it takes to navigate the mountains and molehills that you have had to climb and traverse in life. Many people can be strong when life is easy, but when something big happens, they don't know how to handle it, and they often make the wrong choices.
>
> I saw that inner strength in your mom as well, since her accident. Maybe you got that from her. You have been there for her when she needed someone, and now she is there for you. What we give to others often comes back to us.
>
> I hope you know that you have the strength to walk down a healthy path. It is your choice. I am one of your biggest fans from afar.

*February 7, 2019*

My friend's husband was diagnosed with Alzheimer's. His driver's license had been taken away, and they needed to make a lot of adjustments to their daily routines. Knowing that things were going to get worse wasn't easy. When your partner has taken good care of you over the years, assuming responsibility for most things, it can be a very eye-opening reality. She has been a quick study throughout this difficult time. I admire her tenacity and her self-awareness.

> *Grace:* so often I come back to this word. When we most need the Holy Spirit, he sends a lot of grace our way. It seeps into our bone marrow. We can choose to acknowledge it and use it for our immediate situation, or we can channel it into other things like trust, wisdom, faith, strength, and courage. That is what I see us doing. You are living your life with grace. You have learned to trust and receive the peace that comes with it. You are listening with a very keen ear and gaining wisdom every day. Your already strong faith has grown tremendously in love and acceptance.
>
> Your strength and courage have made you more self-confident. If you don't know the answers, you have the strength to find them. If your questions are physical or spiritual, you listen from the deepest part of you and learn the lesson, knowing that the answer will be okay. You bring

joy into your life by sharing your peace with others, and you trust the peace you've found within yourself.

It is a time of constant change and challenge, and I have never seen you in a better place. When you experience negativity, you know how to exit from it with peace and courage. Your journey is moving quickly, and I love that I get to see it. I know eventually things will slow down, but the beautiful part is that all of these words will stay with you.

*April 19, 2019*

My friend was planning to make some major changes in her life. She seemed to be inspired to do so, and this awakening of her spirit was beautiful to witness. I have always been inspired by her strength and grace.

> This time of year always gets my juices going. We have lived through the cold and gray days of winter with all its ice and snow. The hibernation of the trees without leaves has played heavily on our souls. But I love the awakening that spring evokes with the celebration of the Eucharist, and then the depths of the suffering, injustice, and death that ultimately brings us the glorious resurrection.
>
> The Easter season begins, and it is so full of hope and light and new growth. By the time we get to Pentecost, we have reached the top of the mountain. We have received an abundance of grace, and we want to share it with everyone around us. It is such a meaningful journey each year, and although it is different for each of us, I love to experience it. I love to reflect on previous times. I love to relive the lessons that I learned and the joys that I celebrated.
>
> My wonderful friend, welcome to your awakening and your reawakening. I love our

time together, and I do my best to consume the wisdom you share to make it a part of my heart, my soul, and my mind. You are refreshing. You are so caring. On Holy Thursday, we all chanted, "Jesus, remember me when you come into your kingdom." That is how you live every moment of your life. Isn't that what we all want? As always, I come away from my time spent with you feeling awed and inspired. You remind me to be my best self, whatever that looks like. The grace you have been given is so beautiful, and you never waste an ounce. You are always recycling it to others so they can do the same.

I wish you the best in all of your new ventures. Your intimate relationship with the Holy Spirit directs you from within, and the year ahead will be amazing. This awakening year will be something to experience. We will have to wait and see what it will look like. Happy Easter and Happy Spring!

*May 2, 2019*

This friend of mine was going through many things at the same time. She was healing from an accident and her recovery was going to take years. Her son had been diagnosed as bipolar, and she wasn't getting much support from friends and family. She still has neuropathy, and they aren't sure if she will ever be completely out of pain. He is young, so it is difficult to figure the path or the passion for his life.

> This morning, I was thinking about my favorite word, *grace,* and wondering why it is my favorite word. My first thought was of ballerinas and the beauty and grace of their movements, how they move their arms and straighten their legs and make it so mesmerizing. Then, I thought there is more to it than that—and absolutely there is. It is the link that we have to God and to the Holy Spirit. I need grace to receive courage when I need it. I need grace to alleviate my fears, either real or imagined. I need grace for enlightenment. Does it make any sense to you?
>
> I pray that you will freely accept the grace that is available to you every day. I wish I could make the decision for you, but I can't. Just like I can't make someone lose weight or stop smoking. It is a decision that has to come from you.

So, my amazing, wonderful friend, do something for yourself. Notice the light around you that makes it easier for you to see, and when you are ready, support your son and accept your own journey back to physical health.

When was the last time that you smiled? You have the most beautiful smile, but I never see it. When was the last time you laughed with your heart, body, and soul? I haven't seen that either. You have the most joyous laugh, and it always made me smile. I miss that person, the one who lived life fully. Your constant worry is going to break your body and soul. Save yourself. Come out of the darkness and into the light. I know you don't know what the next step will bring, but have faith and let it unfold. You may find glory. Every day will not be perfect, but with grace, you can bridge that gap.

Consider making a change in your daily prayer. Pray for grace, and the Holy Spirit will give you what you need for that moment and for that day. You are strong for everyone else—be strong for yourself. You are worth the effort.

I will share some of my grace with you today so that you are full of grace. I can spare some, and there isn't anyone I would rather give it to. I hope you will feel the Holy Spirit surrounding you and keeping your steps light and airy. And I pray that the Holy Spirit keeps you in the palm of his hands. My prayer is that you love you as much as I do.

*May 7, 2019*

My friend's husband was ill and she assumed most of the caregiving responsibilities. He had made irrational decisions with their retirement money without her knowledge. Although the money issues have been resolved, the caregiving duties have expanded.

I have been thinking a lot about grace lately. It is our bridge to whatever we need at any given time. Sometimes we need forgiveness, or wisdom, compassion, love. You have compassion built into your DNA, so you don't need grace for that. Grace provides the bridge that gives us the strength we need at just the right moment, courage to face the future, and wisdom to find the path. We are so blessed to be given grace in these situations. I have started to include that in my daily prayers. God, give me grace for whatever I need today. So that is my prayer for you also. I pray you receive the extra grace that you need this week. Use it however you need it.

I am so grateful to have you in my life. You have strength of character, a wonderful sense of humor, and amazing compassion. I love that you never stop learning. The lessons that you learn stay with you and become a part of your life. You are beautiful, kind, and loving. I believe that God has given you an abundance of grace, and you never squander it. You use every last drop and that makes me care for you even more. You keep moving forward, even when that next step is often tough. We all want to be full of grace, and you are well on your way.

*January 21, 2020*

This was a young gal just ending her twenties and changing jobs, changing cities, and moving up in her profession. She was inspiring to me. She started this new job and within a couple of months, they were already promoting her. I love seeing her talent and sharing her successes.

> Thank you for the most delightful and lovely evening. It was so kind of you after a long day at work to give me the whole evening.
>
> I can't help but think of courage when I think of you. You have the courage to change jobs, to change cities, to have faith in yourself and in your abilities to stand out in a situation. Wow! I can't help but notice people who are carving their life in a very active way. I know how talented you are and how willing you are to learn and figure a way through the maze of retail. It is an ever-changing world, and I believe you will be progressive and observant to recognize the changes early. You are bright and you are beautiful. You are kind and you are loyal. All of those will work well for you in life.
>
> As we start out this year, but really this decade, I can't help but wonder how different your life will look at the end of it. I have to believe it will be good. It isn't that there won't be

pitfalls or pain, but with your courage that always gives you strength, you will weather any storm.

I love that you have great role models in your profession. When you meet them or read about them, you try to emulate some of their qualities. So many people don't dare to dream. You have always been a goal-setting person, and the goals change as your life changes. You don't get bogged down in what you thought it would be like, but what it could be like now. That is such an attribute.

I am truly amazed at the courage you have to see the real you. I find that at a young age, it is difficult to know who you really are. To selfishly love yourself, warts and all, allows you have the energy and the will to love others It takes courage to see the great parts of yourself and pat yourself on the back, as well as to see the parts that you would like to change. By doing that and being honest with yourself, good things happen. You are able to make the tough decisions and then take the next step in life.

Your kindness is so apparent. Knowing who you are always gives you the ability to be kind and help others find their way. You can give a hand up along the way. Those random acts of kindness make such a big difference in the world. Many times you don't realize the impact on someone's life, but I have found that kindness always makes a difference.

You are so loyal. You have so many friends from grade school through college and beyond. People are so important in our lives. Some stay friends for a short time and some for life, but I have found them all to be very important.

I know the Holy Spirit is always walking beside you, helping you to see the light in the darkness, and the even brighter light in the light. He helps us make the choices for ourselves, and to be our best selves.

I find you amazing with that wonderful quality of kindness. Be true to you, and then life seems to take care of itself.

*January 30, 2020*

I wrote this letter to my friend whose husband has cancer. He has been through many rounds of chemo and has had several surgeries. Through it all, they managed to find joy in every day knowing that their time together is limited. Both are an inspiration to me. Living fully, one day at a time, isn't easy.

> Being that *grace* is my favorite word, I am so happy that I can use it with you in mind. We had such a wonderful time last night. I enjoyed your wonderful hospitality and then the delicious meal and the time we spent sharing. I love being with both of you. You are such good people.
>
> You have walked through life surrounded by grace. I believe that we are given a certain amount of grace each day to do with it whatever we choose. Sometimes we use it to find courage or strength, love or kindness or compassion. We can use whatever we need each day, knowing we'll receive more the next day. When we use grace to help ourselves, it becomes part of us and allows us to share it with others. I think you receive more than most. I see how you share it with those around you and how you use it for yourself when you need it most.

I have been praying for you and for your spouse on my morning walks. I will continue to keep you close to my heart and in my prayers. You are very special, and I know how wonderful you are. You are surrounded by friends who are an important part of your journey. I know you are reticent to share your thoughts and fears with the world, but I hope that you will share them with your closest friends. When you cry, remember that tears are healing. Any emotion that brings you to tears allows the healing and relief to begin.

You are a wonderful wife and caregiver, and your husband is considerate and grateful. I love knowing you as a couple and as individuals. You truly care about the other.

I am so glad that I met you and have gotten to know you and have been inspired by the grace that you share. You see people with all their flaws, but you don't judge them. You understand that we all have imperfections, but we try to do the best we can. With grace, it is easier to make good choices.

Be sure to take good care of yourself. I always seem to pray for the caregiver, because I think it is so hard to watch a loved one suffer. You have been responsible for keeping your husband as healthy as possible. I know he knows it and is grateful, and I hope he lets you know. You are a treasure, a really sparkling treasure. Love yourself like we love you, and certainly like God loves you.

# What Would You Have Me Do Today, Lord?

*I have this friend whose mother was dying by inches. She was in some pain and bedridden. Every day she woke up and was a bit disappointed that she was still here. So she would start every morning with "What would you have me do today, Lord?" Then there would come inspiration to pray for or call someone and wish them well. She could do very little, but she still tried to make a difference while still in this world. I can't help but think that Jesus was very happy to meet her in the next life. That phrase has stayed with me. In our busy lives, we forget that maybe we are supposed to help someone in the smallest of ways or the biggest of ways every day. If we start our day asking that question, we always find someone who could use our help, if only to listen for a few moments.*

—Theresa V

# 5

## COMPASSION

*April 1, 2014*

I wrote this to a gal I had worked with for many years. I was retiring, and I just wanted to thank her for the wonderful moments that we had shared. She is an amazing person, and I wanted her to know I saw that in her.

> Well, my sweet, beautiful, talented, wonderful good friend, I will miss you. I love your honesty, your willingness to improve yourself every day, your energy, your sense of humor, your kindness, your love of nature, and your love for your dog. You have been through so much in the last few years, starting with the healthiest person I know having to journey through breast cancer, having your immune system crash, and the ski accident. Then you changed your diet and lifestyle, rebuilt your immune system, recharged your batteries, and became once again the energizer bunny. All through everything, you never felt sorry for yourself. *Why me?* You didn't complain about the pain, and you were always looking at the next step back to recovery. The lemons you got always turned into lemonade—organic of course.
>
> The Holy Spirit wraps his arms around you, surrounding you with his love and his goodness, and I love to see it come through you. You are so kind and nurturing, and a loyal friend. But

mostly, you are always helping people when they need you the most. I loved our talks in the morning before the rest of the people got there. You have such a big heart and so many people are the recipients of the love and goodness that comes directly from you.

I will miss you and hope to see you even with your busy schedule. I wish you peace and peace for your family.

*August 4, 2014*

This is a very special person that I met at a journaling group. She always was a light in the room, and I couldn't wait until she shared her thoughts. She had a very busy schedule, so she couldn't always be there. You could feel her compassion, and she was busy taking care of people with so much joy. She did write me back, and she said she contacted our friend to help her.

> Well, my spiritual friend, I have thought about writing this letter for a very long time and finally decided to get on with it and stop just thinking about it.
>
> When I think of you, I think of wisdom. You have so much to give to people. You always say that you don't write, but when you speak, it is as if you are reciting a poem. Your pauses and your flow of words are beautiful. I wish I had a tape recorder so I could write your words and let you see your "writings."
>
> You have wonderful compassion and are open to accepting people as they are, not who you think they should be. That can be so difficult for many of us. Our egos can get in the way, but you do not let yours rule and that is rare.
>
> When I saw you talking to our friend the other day, I could really see that you were her person to help with her spiritual direction. You

might not have the official title, but you have that in your very being. I hope you have time to meet with her for some meaningful conversations. She is so in need of a good listener with some simple wisdom to help her set some priorities.

You always uplift me, and I always come away with a nugget that is amazing. I am in awe and many times blessed to have met you and have gotten to know you.

*November 6, 2014*

When I met her in class, she really just touched my heart. She had this amazing passion for love of God, and she wanted to spread this love to the world. She has so much energy. When I run into her, I always can feel the fire within her.

> *Wow*, you are amazing. I normally have this beautiful dove circling my head with wonderful words for people in a very loving way. I sit down and write a letter and everything is beautiful. Then I met you, and my life shifted. I woke up in the middle of the night with an urgency that I have never felt before. I can only refer to the experience I had last night as my Pentecost. I was baptized into the fire. Your passion, compassion, love, humility, innocence, obedience, and kindness blew me away. The gift you were given by the Holy Spirit isn't given to very many people because they would abuse the power. I looked into your eyes, and I saw your soul. It was open and beautiful and committed. I tell you, when you put your hand on my heart, it literally stopped, and when it started again, I felt courage, I felt love, and I felt empowered.
>
> The impact that you have on people isn't subtle. However, it is life-changing in a moment. Don't shy away from it and try not to sec-

ond-guess yourself. The Holy Spirit is putting these people in your life. You have a fire in you that should not be quenched because it is based in obedience and love. Your tears are so beautiful, and never be ashamed of them. They are a part of you, so just embrace them. They come from such a deep compassion and caring. I felt like you were in my mind, body, and soul, and it felt great. I knew I was in good hands.

The aura around you changes the tones of the colors to a brightness that is piercing. Keep your mission and use your amazing gift. You are fearless, and we need you to light our fires and take us out of our comfort zones and to places where God wants us to be.

*September 29, 2016*

This was a manicurist that I had seen a few times; her husband was just diagnosed with cancer. She touched me with her story. It is three years later and he is still alive, but after several surgeries and chemo, the road hasn't been easy, but I still see her strength and courage and love throughout this. She has changed so much during this time, and all for the better.

> It has been on my heart for a while to write you a letter. I kept thinking it wasn't the right time and would put those words in my head down for a nap. But as often happens, they come back and so now it is time. Here is my letter.
>
> First, I want you to know how much I look forward to seeing you and talking to you when my nails are more than a mess. I love to find people who do their jobs so well, so thanks for all of the great service. I love your sense of humor and the way you look at the world. I felt a connection from the beginning.
>
> I love to hear about your life. I believe that you are a person who has a tremendous amount of courage. You take on very difficult things and meet them head-on. I hear how you raise your family and you instinctively know what is best for each child. You take their heartache and their strengths, and you help them to take the next

step. Now, as you husband journeys through cancer, you're helping him along the path. It takes great courage right now as well as strength. I know that you know that the Holy Spirit is surrounding you with his love and support. Learn to lean into it. He will help you. This is no small thing that has been put before your family, and it is imperative that you surround yourself with positive air and positive people. I think it is great that you are going to church again, and being in a small Bible group can give you much peace. Please don't forget to take care of yourself. You can't give what you don't have, so remember that you need to be nourished.

I don't know what is down the road because we are only promised today, but that is why we need to live each day the best that we know how. I have found that if you start with gratitude, even with the smallest of things, it brings love and peace into the day somehow.

*December 30, 2016*

This was written to a gal whom I met again after many years. We reconnected and started walking together, and the stories she shared touched my heart. She had great compassion. It struck me that she didn't see it in herself, so I wrote this letter to her to try to help her see her goodness in the way she took care of others.

I was inspired to write you a letter after all of the sharing that we have done during our walk. These words and these letters just come to me, so it is always best if I get them on paper.

Believe me, I know we all have flaws and all we can do is to try to work on them. But today I want to tell you what is so good about you and what makes you so very unique and special. These words are given to you in love, from me and, more importantly, from the Holy Spirit.

I see compassion as being the very essence of you. You look at the world from eyes that care and need to help people who really need your support. You are there for anyone in a crisis. Friend or stranger can be calling you, and there you come with your beautiful smile, in a bit of a shy way, but with true understanding of what is needed. You don't wear this with a badge, and you don't do it for the credit; you just help people from your heart and from your soul. I think that is your gift. It gives you joy to be that quiet rock for people to lean on. It comes with grace and with true kindness.

I know you are planning to make changes to your life, and we will see what they are. Whatever they will be, you will be at the right place at the right time. I know that your compassion will be part of the story. Compassion is something I struggle with, so I always am in awe when I see it in others. I love to see the beauty and the naturalness in you, and I love to experience it through your eyes. I know you don't see how special this is, but it makes you special, and it is an amazing thing for me to see.

After many years of marriage, this friend's husband wanted a divorce. He became very ill and needed constant care. She was there for his treatment, and it finally worked. I walked with her throughout this journey with many letters and saw a wonderful transformation of her soul, body, and mind. She taught me so much with her struggles.

> You have been on my mind since it is hard to see you with your 24/7 commitment. I have heard you saying very gentle questions to him, and I want you to know that you inspire me. You have allowed yourself to let your best self come to the foreground in this tough situation. It is so true that when you need it the most, you are walking with God and there is only one set of footprints. He has you in his loving arms.
>
> I don't see it often, but your strength alone is beyond. What goes along with this is courage, faith, compassion, and love. You love yourself enough to not let this adversity change your beautiful, caring self. I know you feel the anger and the injustice, but this will work out. You know your God and He knows you, and in the scheme of life that is most important.
>
> You were so kind to me when I was brand new to this community. Your loving spirit was immediately apparent to me, so I thank you for

giving me the courage to introduce myself to others.

I think you have that wonderful gift of compassion. I see it in your love of dogs and your interest in wildlife. I believe people are good and kind, but so many stop at the action part. This takes so much more time, energy, passion, and commitment. Along with your compassion and encouragement, you have the fortitude to make it all happen.

You have taken your health issues in stride and learned to live your best life. Just remember to take care of yourself in this chaos. Your needs are not inconsequential. Let people help you if you need a break. You are not alone.

*February 5, 2018*

This was a friend of mine who was caring for a sick husband. They were having marital problems as well. Things worked out, but this was a very tough couple of years. It was amazing to see how she cared for him when there were so many things going on with them. Sometimes, when you are brought to your knees, you learn how to become close to God and learn the lessons that were always just out of reach.

> I think compassion is your main gift. You shared that story with me the other day about your aunt, and I could see the joy in your eyes that you could take care of her in her later years. We often think of these gifts and discount them with, "Well, I really liked her." But when it is your gift, it comes easily and gives you great joy. I am sure you could make a list of many people who have received your compassion. When people are sent to you, you don't let them down.
>
> Even though these are trying times in your marriage, and there is much resentment and anger at the choices that he is making, you take care of him with beautiful compassion. You are learning so much from all of these medical personnel, and it will help you along this journey and maybe other ones as well.

I have so much admiration for you and others that have this beautiful gift. With this gift from the Holy Spirit, he will continue to send you people who need your kindness and caring. You won't have to search for them. Please know how special that makes you. I love your curiosity to learn. I know the people you encounter will be forever changed.

*November 29, 2018*

This is a gal whom I worked with but hadn't seen for a while. She had a great sense of humor and was someone you could depend on to be there for you if you needed help. She had had a sometimes difficult relationship with her mom over the years. But when it was near the end of her mom's life, she was all in and took great care of her. She even had her living with her for a time. It was two full-time jobs that left little time for anything, much less sleep.

> I am so sorry to hear the news of your mom's passing. She sure did live her life on her terms, and she even died on her terms. She died before the holidays so as not to disrupt yours. Of course, I know you will be thinking of her all during the season and after as well.
>
> I look at your mom and think she really did well in her long life. How many of us get to live on our own in our home until the age of ninety? She was strong, she had determination, and she could be feisty, but she had a good sense of humor. I think she passed some of that on to the favorite daughter, you. I love that she realized what a treasure you are. I love that she experienced your caring and love, and she gave them both back to you. I love that you were there for her when she needed love and support. You gave it freely with no strings attached, and you helped

make her last years ever so much more meaningful than they would have been.

It is a funny thing about moms and dads; we miss them terribly, no matter the age. I know after fifteen years, I still think of mine and usually with gratitude for something she taught me. I am so glad I was able to see her strength, her faith, her resilience. I know you have those same kinds of feelings. The memories stay and the smiles come after the original sadness leaves. You are a such a good daughter and person, and I love to see how you live your life with integrity. You put your life on hold more than once, loss of sleep with sundowners' syndrome, took the time in the hospital, rehab, doctors' appointments, breakfasts out. That, my friend, is true love. Your mom saw it and felt it and so needed it at that point in her journey. I think you were her champion, her guardian angel, her friend, her memory. You were such a gift to her. I know the patience you had, and when the others were running away from her, you were running toward her. Sometimes you think you were less than, but I can tell you that you were more than. Your heart overflows, and it lands right where it is supposed to be.

*June 13, 2019*

This is a gal who is realizing her marriage isn't what she had expected. She has some very real health issues that take up a great deal of her time. She always amazes me with her strength. I feel so bad that she has this constant pain. My nickname for her in my heart is "Amazing Grace" because that is always what I see in her.

> I am constantly humbled and inspired every time I see you. You have so many things on your plate and they may overwhelm you, but they never beat you. You accept the rhythm of your household, although it doesn't usually have any of your input. You are met with silence and anger, and it isn't what you are in any way. I think it is why it brings you up short when you feel some of those feelings. You have always over-given yourself to so many people.
>
> Now, in your need, so many move away from you. They think it is too much for you to ask. You are in pain, and it is a big deal. You are giving your all to this healing that is long and extremely hard and painful. I am amazed by your wisdom. You take every bit of information you hear or find and make it work for you. You are never afraid to learn, to listen, to feel. You have had so many real trials mixed in with a pretty

good life. This test is the toughest one you have had, I think.

Trusting the Holy Spirit to take care of your son because he is a man now and needs to make his choices good and bad isn't easy with your "I can fix this" personality. I know this is so hard to take a back seat. I know that you can't do this on your own, and I know the Holy Spirit will give you the grace to have the strength and courage to see this through.

Life has a way of bringing spectacular new beginnings when we have been in the deepest of ditches. I love that you are learning to use your voice where it is needed. Your words are making a difference in people's lives, and when you can't believe I said that, you know the Holy Spirit is within you. I know that your life is going to change and I don't know how, but you are going to experience true happiness. Thank you, my unique friend, for always leaving me with little more pep in my step and a lot more love and inspiration in my heart. Love yourself. Forgive your flaws. Rejoice in your amazing gifts. Use your voice for the good of the people who will hear. Let the Holy Spirit guide you.

# Don't Mess with the Holy Spirit

*I was taking a class with a few women, and each week we would meet and there would always be a lesson to be learned. One week, a gal who was sharing had some doubt on how her situation would be resolved. My friend said, "Don't mess with the Holy Spirit." That was a lesson we all loved, and that phrase came up often in our discussions. Knowing that life can sometimes bring you lemons, if you just remember, don't mess with the Holy Spirit, you have it covered. He is on your side and he will help you through the bad times and the good times. When things look precarious, that phrase will pop into my mind and I know to just keep plodding along. I don't need to be in total control of every situation. It also comes up when something unusual happens. I think, what a coincidence, but then I think with a smile on my face: "Don't mess with the Holy Spirit and I go on my way."*

—Ann Marie K

# 6

## FAITH

*February 11, 2015*

After many years of marriage, my friend was going through a divorce. She was blindsided by the situation, and it had been difficult for a while, but she was picking up the pieces of her life and starting anew. She began putting her many talents and gifts to work. Now, five years later, her life looks very different. She continues to try new things and is open to change. She has a very strong faith and she teaches others to know themselves, love themselves, and to be true to who they are. She has been a huge blessing in my life.

> I haven't been feeling well, and so I have been homebound for a while. I was praying that I'd find the words for a letter for you, and when I woke, I saw your face and the words were there. I am grateful that I can write you, my teacher, my mentor, and yes, my friend.
>
> There are so many changes going on in your life. Selling your house and moving to a new city and community is a huge step, but I feel strongly that it is the right one. It is totally your place, and you are free to begin a whole new life and make all new memories. I see beautiful fireworks in your future, along with glorious sunrises and sunsets. The quiet with the spectacular is a great combination. Your aura is brighter than ever.
>
> I was thinking of you while I was listening to a Christian radio station on the radio, and

they kept repeating this phrase, "You have God's favor." It is so true. I know you are going to love your new life and appreciate your new home. I wish I could give you specifics, but one thing I know for sure, it will be beyond your dreams. God has amazing things in store for you. He spoke loudly to you, so you would know he was present at the toughest times. Now, he is whispering to you every day and giving you direction. You know how to listen, to ask, to communicate, and to act. What more can God want from any of us? You spread love wherever you go, and that is the most important thing. The two commandments that Jesus taught us are "love God" and "love your neighbor." You have committed to that, and they are your starting point in everything you do.

You have a wonderful spirit, and you are always seeking the truth. Continue on your journey with no fear. You are one of the chosen who has God's favor.

*May 22, 2016*

This friend of mine was graduating from high school. I always thought she was special, and I thought it was time that I let her know. Since then, she has completed college, she has a job, and the possibilities in her life are endless. She is still amazing. I love watching her mature as she spreads joy and goodness wherever she goes.

First of all, congratulations on your graduation from high school. It is a big day to say the least. You may feel some sadness at the thought of leaving the life and friends you have made, but you will experience the joy of a new adventure as you begin your journey through womanhood. It will be the first time you are completely on your own, making choices, and living your life. Hopefully, you will make many more good choices than bad. I have faith that you will.

Speaking of faith, I hope that you will take your faith with you. There is the Trinity, the Father, Son, and the Holy Spirit. Pick one to be your guide to surround you with love and kindness. Coming from a family of all women, Mary, the blessed Mother, has supported me throughout life. She intercedes through her son in my times of need, so don't hesitate to ask her for guidance. There are saints who can guide you as well, so pick a favorite to walk by your side.

I believe we don't walk this earth without help from above. The more you trust in your personal relationship with God, with Mary, and with the saints, the easier your journey will be.

I think it is also important to give back. Even though you will be very busy with school, if you could find one hour a week to volunteer, you will have more clarity and joy in your life. You could work in a community garden, or a soup kitchen. You could work with children, either sick or well. I just think if you find ways to contribute early in life, you will experience more love and joy along the way. With your whole life before you, it is important to set goals. I think it is equally important to live in the moment. It is a tricky road to do both, and you may struggle, but the sooner you learn to balance both, the easier and more satisfying your life will be.

I have always seen and felt a very specialness in you, and I am so happy that you got into a university that fits your personality and goals. I am confident you will take this transition with your usual grace and wisdom. I look at your future and see so many options. I know you will find the one that is best for you.

Have faith in yourself. Know that your wonderful experiences in dance and travel will help you be more aware, and the friendships you've made will help you see situations and people for what and who they are. Follow your gut and your instincts, and that little voice inside you. They will serve you well.

Enjoy this time in college. It is the one time in your life that you can be a little bit selfish. You only have to take care of yourself, and that won't be true for most of your life. I know you have the responsibility to study and get good grades, but there will be many hours that you can just spoil yourself and do and go where you want. You don't have to ask permission. It is kind of a heady thing at first, but it can give you so much joy and even a giggle or two.

I have watched you from afar, but I haven't missed your inner glow and beautiful aura. You have always been amazing and accomplished well beyond your years. You are ahead of the pack with your wonderful sense of self. I think you have been given many gifts, but you have worked hard to be where you are today. Most people haven't been able to accomplish what you have done with dance and so many other things. It says a lot about your character.

Take really good care of yourself. Be safe. Love life. Enjoy the journey. Feel the love that surrounds you from so many people. Know that I am one. Take this next step with confidence and humility. I wish you nothing but the best.

*March 7, 2018*

My friend was nursing her very ill husband back to health. She taught me how difficult it is to have faith when you are living in darkness. Along the way, she learned the lessons she needed to learn, and now she lives in the light with love and kindness surrounding her.

> *Trust.* Those five letters can mean so many things. It is a beautiful day; I trust it won't rain. Or I trust and have faith that no matter what, my life will be fine, enriched, meaningful, and inspired. When each day is a struggle, it is hard to trust that there is a beautiful light at the end of this tunnel of darkness. I know for sure that you are steadfastly walking out of this darkness into the light of love. You feel the love of your family and friends, and you feel the love of God. Unfortunately, the love in your household is not always apparent. Where there should be gratitude for your compassionate care, there is often sarcasm or anger. Please trust that the rewards for you will be many. Everyone pays for their mistakes, and everyone is rewarded for their good works.
>
> It would be so nice to look into that crystal ball to see how long or hard this will be. I wish you could. Some days must feel more than you can handle. I wish your husband could experience the light and change. However, I trust that

eventually you will be fine, and you will flourish. I trust you will find goodness along your path, and your way forward will be colorful and vibrant. I remember the advice someone gave me once: "If you worry, don't pray; but if you pray, don't worry." As you pray, trust in the Holy Spirit. Lean in. Feel his loving arms around you and know he is in your heart. You are a beautiful person, and your heart is filled with love. I trust that will never change.

Have the best day and soak in the love you so deserve that everyone is freely giving you.

*March 11, 2018*

My friend inspires me and almost everyone she meets. She is a talented artist and writer and in her quiet way, she changes people around her. She has a peacefulness about her that you can't help saying, "I want that." Even when you don't understand it completely, you know you want it.

> If there is one word that describes you, it is *faith*. It is so pure and simple with you. I love your quiet and beautiful and strong faith that leads you to the most extraordinary places. You are always open to new faith encounters. It felt like a perfect fit when you accepted the gift and the grace of intercessory prayer. It is so natural that I'm surprised we didn't think of it sooner. You have been busy pastoring and doing beautiful things, so I know you haven't been wasting time.
>
> You have this amazing ability to listen not only to God but to others. When someone is talking about a rather complex thing, you have the ability to understand what they are saying and explain it simply. I can almost see the wheels turning in your brain. When God puts something in your heart, you listen, you meditate and you walk cautiously down the path. You don't walk out of fear, as others might, but you stay focused and keep moving, led by the eyes of our

Lord. When we're practicing spiritual journaling, your responses from the sharing always reflect the most in-depth understanding. Please keep the innocent, pure, and simple view you have of the world and, at some point many years down the road, take it to your next life where you will rest in the loving arms and light of our God and Savior and Creator.

Thank you, my beautiful friend, for the insight you have shared with me over the years and for allowing me to see the beautiful light that always surrounds you. The Holy Spirit never leaves your side because you are truly one of the chosen.

*April 22, 2018*

My friend's son was diagnosed with a very serious mental illness. It was a tough road for all to travel. Although it's still not easy, they have come a very long way. My friend has learned the true meaning of trust. She has learned to trust her actions and her judgments. Knowing who you are and what you need to do in a situation takes a lot of strength. She has learned to step back and let things happen.

> Trust is so important. First of all, take a breath and trust that you can take the next one. I somehow think you haven't breathed in months or maybe years, so try it. It is refreshing. I believe you are going to make best friends with this word, *trust,* because the situation you are facing is bigger than you. You are a solution-oriented person, and you alone will not be able to solve this puzzle. Trust that your marriage and your family will survive this. Have faith that the Holy Spirit has your son in the palms of his hands and he is surrounding him with his love. Trust that your son feels that love and is able to respond. So, my friend, breathe and trust.
>
> I want to share something that happened to me a week ago. I know I've told you my mantra that baby steps count. Believing that has served me well. My friend's mother was slowly dying. She was bedridden and tired of living, but every

morning, she thought to herself, "I am awake and I am still alive. What would you have me do today?"

I think that is a great way to look at life. Dear Lord, what would you have me do today? In your case, I think the answer is "breathe and trust."

Enjoy your day. Take care of yourself. Do something simple that brings you pleasure. Eat one of your favorite foods. Breathe and trust, trust and breathe. Having faith is so important in difficult times. You can do this, and your son is going to receive the help he needs.

*March 16, 2019*

I wrote this letter to a friend who had asked her husband for a divorce. When the reality sets in, it wasn't always easy for her to accept what her new life looked like. It takes time and faith and a lot of energy to create a new life, and there were times when she felt the panic of her decision.

> Calm. If you could just hold tightly to that word. I know when you are in the midst of a storm, it is hard to remember what calm feels like. If only you could keep things calm until everyone gets accustomed to the new look for your family. Even though things will be different, it doesn't mean they will be worse for everyone. I think it is so important to keep communications as open as possible. Continue to be aware of all that's happening, and if you feel like you can't trust what's happening, at least be open to listening.
>
> Divorce is never an easy road, but it always is a learning experience, and you will feel yourself grow. After all is said and done, you will gain a lot of wisdom. So keep as calm as possible throughout the process. It might not be easy, but it will be beneficial. You are protective of your girls and rightly so. Their well-being is your primary goal as you navigate this path. I pray that you and your husband share this goal.

You are such a wonderful person, and so I hate to see you suffer in any way. I know that when we are at our weakest, the Holy Spirit is our strength. Lean in as much as you can. He will always be with you when you need Him.

I have found that the more people you share your new circumstances with, the more comfortable you become. As your new life starts taking shape, remember that all of these baby steps count. Pray to be calm. It will help with sleep so you can remain healthy. Many people get ill when their life is in crisis. Stress causes so much grief psychologically as well as physically. I hope this week has no more negative surprises. I pray for you and wish you well. I loved walking by your side and sharing this time with you. You are moving forward, although at times you'll feel like you are standing still or even going backward. The good news is, you will get to your destination. Have faith and be calm.

*June 15, 2019*

My friend is changing her outlook on life. She intended to change many aspects of her life, and we'll have to wait and see if she is successful. She is beginning to know who she really is, and she is liking the person she is becoming. That is a huge step. She has found her voice, and I don't see her losing it ever again. She has also been dealing with several painful health issues, and she is not through the woods yet. I am in constant awe of how lovingly she leads her life.

> Your life is about to change. The Holy Spirit is giving you your voice, and He will send the right people to you for your healing. I wish your son could hear your voice, but he can't right now. It will be someone else's voice that will bring him forward and reawaken his spirit. You can trust it will happen at just the right time.
>
> Your brother said you saved his life with the words you shared with him. That will start to happen more and more in the life you are creating for yourself. New people will come into your life, and some in your current circle of friends will drop away. Your life will evolve with new friends who need to hear your words.
>
> As you begin this new direction, be aware of your path. The Holy Spirit will be walking with you every step of the way. You won't be as involved as you are now in the constant care

of your son, and with the guidance of the Holy Spirit, you will find new opportunities. Be his faithful servant and he won't disappoint. He will enrich your life beyond recognition. This journey has been a rocky one; it is about to become smoother. He will reward you for your goodness throughout the years.

You will be an inspiration to the people in your life, and you will know exactly what to say to guide them. Trust and have faith. You will be rewarded for your goodness. The time is now, and it is going to be quite a ride. Good luck, my friend.

# You Are Right Where You

# Are Supposed to Be

*I have a friend who had a necklace given to her with the words "You are right where you are supposed to be." She wore it every day as a reminder that there is no need to be rushing with anxiety. It takes away the "coulda shoulda woudas" of the day. Living in the moment, taking care of, and seeing what is happening right now gives you a sense of peace that you can't buy. We often think that we should be at point B when we are still working on point A. If you know you are right where you are supposed to be, you will get to point B at exactly the right time. That phrase can be a de-stresser, and I think of it often. During difficult times, it helps to know that there must be a lesson to be learned at this moment. If this gives you a moment of peace when you need it, you have won the battle.*

—Chris M

# 7

# PEACE

*April 28, 2018*

This was a friend of mine who had a bad car accident and required lengthy rehabilitation and physical therapy to regain use of her arm again. Others in her family also had serious illness, and the stress level was high. It has been a difficult time, but she has found peace in her life.

> This is a cold gray day, but kind of a perfect day to experience peace. My niece taught me that some of the best days are rainy days because there is no pressure. You don't have to do anything or go anywhere. I feel like that in the winter with a big snowfall as well. Just be in your happy place. It could be reading or writing or organizing or cooking. I always remember your wonderful gift of organization. You could look at a drawer or cabinet and think of a better way of organizing it. I am not sure if you have a lot of obligations, but I hope you can take a few minutes and feel some peace sinking into your skin, your bones, your muscles, your bloodstream. It can be healing.
>
> The other thing I always associated with you is your capacity to research things. That can be drudgery for most of us, but for you it is joyful. You always want to completely understand things. Knowledge is power, and it certainly is for you.

Being quiet is the only way I know to feel any kind of peace. You can be doing something, but try to feel peace in your heart. It is so important in this world which is always moving at a fast pace, to stop and feel peace. People forget about peace and serenity. They forget it exists. I think that without it, it's really hard to live in the light. There is always darkness and it can surround us, but the light lifts us up and helps us see the world differently. I love the "Peace be with you" from the mass, so, my friend, I wish that for you. Do something that helps you feel peace because life is supposed to be lived in the light. Luckily, that is not true only on sunny days but gray days too.

*May 5, 2018*

This is a friend who was going through a tough time in her marriage. It took her a while, but she walked through the weeds and into the meadow. It was a difficult journey, but as is so often true, she came out on the other side as a much more spiritual person finding her way in life, right where she was supposed to be.

> I know it is supposed to be the calm before the storm, but what I heard yesterday was calm at the end of the storm. I am so glad that you had time to yourself to refill your spirit and your physical well-being. You are still driving down that rocky road, but your vision is so good that you are missing every pothole. It has been eye-opening for your spouse to see his many wrong choices. That being said, I do trust the Holy Spirit to change someone's heart and mind and spirit. I know that he is grateful for the wonderful care you are giving him, even if he doesn't say it out loud. It is unfortunate that his children aren't there for him in his time of need, so your compassion is so important now.
>
> So I love that you are calm. I love that the anger has dissipated. I know there is sadness there, but that will be rectified in time. You have grown by leaps and bounds in faith, hope and love. You know that your faith is locked and loaded. With

him praying as well, I believe it will make a difference in his life as well as yours.

You have love for yourself and have given and felt all of the love from many people in your tribe. I wish you to have hope and faith and know that all will be better. I think you are living your best life. I was just reading an article on how wonderful it is to go up in a plane and see the beauty that awaits when you get above the clouds. There is brilliant sunlight. I think you have been blessed to see some of the beautiful light in some of the special moments throughout this time. People have sent you as much light and love as they could, and it is so great that you have such an open heart to accept it. Grace has helped getting you through.

*August 25, 2018*

A friend of mine was struggling on whether to save or end a thirty-year marriage. The marriage survived but not without a lot of thought and much work.

> I loved the beautiful conversation we had this morning. Your voice and your demeanor sounded so different. Your heart has opened, it has softened, and it is loving again. You are not a person to hold a grudge, judge others, or live with hatred in your soul. That is why these last two years have been so hard. The injustice was killing your heart and mind and soul with anger and hatred. Everyone believed you were being wronged, but you were worried about being whole again. Being right wasn't giving you any joy or happiness.
>
> I hear your peace when you speak. It is such an important emotion. It says you know your God as well as yourself. It shows you how to live your best life. I see you doing that, taking care of your husband with love and kindness.
>
> Mainly, I am happy because you have righted yourself. We are never alone, and I know the Holy Spirit has got this. The cloud has been lifted and your goodness suits you. Enjoy living in the light and being true to yourself. This jour-

ney really changed you and, most importantly, your relationship with God. I know you will never go backward.

*October 5, 2018*

I wrote this to a friend who was recuperating from an auto accident. With physical therapy, she was trying to get feeling back into her arm one inch at a time. She was overwhelmed and didn't know how to cope.

> Breathe! I keep seeing you hold your breath because you aren't sure what is around the corner. My prayer for you is that you can turn off your brain for one minute and breathe deeply, fill your lungs, and slowly let it out. Just concentrate on breathing. Watch that living breath while exhaling and bring it all back in with inhaling. Breath is life-giving.
>
> I prayed for you with some gentle but fierce thoughts. I wish I could relieve the physical pain and also the intense pain in your heart. But maybe just the breathing will help lesson some of it for at least a few moments. Give some time to this breathing regimen and take yourself to a wonderful, safe place in the arms of the Holy Spirit. Stay there as long as you can with those cleansing breaths.
>
> One breath at a time is the way the day goes. One day at a time is the way life goes. I believe that we get strength with each step we take forward. I believe that the sun will rise tomorrow.

So with one breath, one step, one day, and with the sunshine and warmth, we can mold our life. I hope your pain lessens. I hope your arm heals.

Please take care of yourself because you are precious and you are worth it. Take one breath at a time because that is all that we can do. Learn one lesson at a time because that is all that we can do. Breathe and feel the goodness in your mind, body, and soul.

*June 5, 2019*

This was a neighbor of mine. I was coming back from my walk at seven in the morning and he was leaving for work. He stopped to say hello and we got into this very deep conversation. It stayed with me and I couldn't get it out of my mind. I wrote this letter to him, but it is the only letter that I didn't deliver. I'm not sure why, but I couldn't give it to him.

> You have been on my mind since our short talk the other morning. I loved that you shared your mother-in-law's story. I couldn't help but realize that she is a person who has found that total inner peace. I have met people like that and I know my reaction to them was the same as yours and everyone who comes in contact with them. I want what they have. I know you said you were not a believer and I can respect that. But I thought I would share with you a very simple thing I do every day. I just say, "Come, Holy Spirit." I don't know what I will be facing each day, but I have found, as the day unfolds, I see things and hear things with more clarity. The birds singing in the morning sound fabulous. The luscious green of the lawns and the trees are spectacular. The people I meet are kinder and are always interesting. It is simple and only takes a second. So try it,

even if you don't believe. It can't hurt. See what happens.

I love talking to you and hearing the stories you have up your sleeve. You are such a great story teller that I am focused to the end. I can see the goodness in you as well as the kindness. I think your love of music and your talent of playing have helped you see the good things in life. There are so many good people in this world, and you are certainly one of them.

You know the journey to that real peace can start in so many ways from sadness, fear, anxiety, or happiness. But, eventually, I think, you have to get to joy which is deeper than happiness, love which involves everyone, then to that beautiful peace that is within. It allows not only acceptance but also comfort and calmness that is beyond stress. It takes you beyond the craziness of life.

Good luck with my three-word prayer, "Come Holy Spirit." Great to see you as always, and with the good weather coming, I am sure I will see you more.

*January 6, 2020*

This was a gal who I met in my travels. I looked forward to seeing her and being with her amazing sense of peace that always surrounded her.

> *Peace,* I love that word. It is in my top two favorite words, with *grace* being my favorite. It is something that we all strive for, but few of us get. I know that I have met very few who really have it. When I meet someone like you, I have always said to myself, "I want that." I didn't have a word for that but finally thought I could replace the word *that* with the word *peace* and it fits perfectly. You live in the moment. You are non-judgmental and, being at peace with yourself, you allow people to be who they are in that moment of time.
>
> I have noticed, when visiting here, that you are the moral compass of this community, from teaching yoga, showing people how to relax and strengthen themselves, to leading the Bible study that includes listening and sharing and growing.
>
> I wonder if you were always that way, or did you learn it along the way? Living on a boat for seven years, as you did, could teach that, I suppose. There are so many very unique experiences. I choose to think that you can get there from happiness and joy, but that is my optimistic self.

Many find it through hardship and tragedy. All I know is that few get there in a timely fashion.

I thank you for being one of the few I have met who have peace, and you are a peacemaker as well. You are a joy to me, and you soothe the multitudes. People follow you and listen to you and take your words to heart.

I loved your short gratitude prayer at our dinner. Particularly at our age, we can dwell on the things we have lost. It takes that quiet little nudge from you to remind us of the things we have gained, such as wisdom, closeness to our God, love, caring, compassion. You have all of that wrapped in one word, *peace*. You are a treasure to your family and to all of the extended families that you have. I hope that you know your worth and that you lead by example. So many of us are saying the same thing, "I want that" or "I want peace." Thanks for showing me what it looks like in you.

*January 20, 2020*

This was written to a friend of mine getting through another Michigan winter. They can seem to go on forever with the ever-present gray skies. She is constantly busy, and it is hard for her to slow down. She has so many obligations for others that sometimes I wish she will just pause and take care of her needs.

> Being snowed in can be relaxing, industrious, aggravating, or peaceful. I love when you can't get outside because of weather. The choices are limited, but they are all good. You can do nothing but watch TV or read a book. You can sleep later and longer. You can clean the refrigerator and be happy that something looks great knowing that it never would have gotten done otherwise. I love the occasional rainy or snowy day because it slows me down and lets me think without distractions. I hope one of those pleasant things happened to you over the weekend.
>
> I am afraid that you will get those ever-present winter blues that jump out of nowhere. I hope that you aren't getting discouraged about your life and all of the obligations that seem to assault you on a daily basis.
>
> My suggestion is to take a few moments and remember who you are on the inside. You are love. Please start by loving yourself. Remember

how far along in your journey you are, and the good changes in your family. Remember the wonderful changes in your spiritual life. You know who you are and you know where you are going. You know where you have been and you aren't going back. There is always trepidation into the unknown, but I know you will be fine. Know that the Holy Spirit has your back. One thing I know for sure is that winter has an end and spring always begins. There is always light and new growth.

I leave you with three words that I read today. Truth: Know that the main truth of life is love. That is who you are, so recognize it in yourself. Beauty: The beauty of your spirit is coming alive. Goodness: Everyone sees that in you. Be good to yourself, and the goodness overflows into the world around you. I like those three words: *truth, beauty,* and *goodness.* I am keeping them close to my heart for a bit. If you want to borrow them, be my guest.

*April 29, 2020*

This was written to a friend of mine during the stay at home phase of the coronavirus pandemic. Given some time to reflect, she took that time to go deep within and see her authentic self and see and feel the Divine within her. She came face to face with her flaws but also with her glories. This was exhausting but also exhilarating.

There is never the miracle of birth without the hours of labor. When we see our baby for the first time, all of the tough times to get there are erased from the pure joy of meeting him for the first time.

The awakening is the most extraordinary experience. With each step of this journey, you are closer to the spectacular light of the universe. When you are on this search for your core, you can't help but experience the glorious power of the Holy Spirit within you. Giving of yourself to love yourself, you find the real source of love. It can't help but be the most extraordinary experience. It is an out-of-body, bright-lights calmness that you didn't know existed. When you slow your breathing and your being, you will become one with your God. Revelations come to the surface that you won't believe. By walking the rocky road, you cross over to the smooth sailing. Once the sins have been forgiven by you, they can be forgotten. Once the anger flows out of your body, there is calm. Experience the enlightenment, the peace, and the bright lights. Experience the wonderful relationship of your body, mind, and soul. They are working in unison. The way is clear and concise. The reward is so worth the rocky road to get there.

So many people don't get to where you are. They go through life racing or just ignoring the riches that are just beyond their grasp. You have the intelligence, the open heart, the love that is always with you. Redirecting that love to you has been the challenge. I know you can do it. I am anxious to hear the outcome. Self-awareness and self-awakening are beyond. It isn't about the surface stuff, but it is about the deep stuff. Your life has been lived to get to this moment.

As happens to me so often when I'm with you, I am in awe. This is the hardest thing you have ever done, and yet you took the first step and then the next. I read a phrase today, "The journey of a thousand miles starts with the first step." You are knocking down walls and I know you won't rebuild them. As always, I wish you didn't have to go through this pain but to get to the splendor it is worth it. The great thing is you will always be able to come back and remember that moment of peace that supersedes everything else around you.

Your future is bright, fun, meaningful, and filled with love and inner peace.

*Relaxation:* I believe you finally get the true meaning of that word because there isn't that inner battle in you. Amazing Grace is your essence.

I am so glad that you will get to see it, respect it, feel it, and know it.

# ACKNOWLEDGMENTS

First of all, I would like to thank Pat Liu and Nancy Walters for helping me with the edit. They were a great help.

Also I would like to thank my many friends that encouraged and inspired me.

Chris A, without her, I would never have found this path. Then Brandin A, Dawn B, Deb B, Kelley B, DJ, Marcia G, Sherry G, Katie F, Judy G, Sonya H, Sharon H, Cindy K, Anne-Marie K, Sue L, Noah L, Chris M, Mary M, Chris P, Mary R, Lori R, Claudia R, Pam R, Carrey S, Karen S, Lauren S, Theresa V, Nancy W, and Nancy W.

Lastly, I would like to thank my family for being the best and bringing me so much happiness. First of all, my husband, Dan, my better half, then my children and grandchildren—Chad and Jessie, Natalie and Isaac, Shannon and Alex, Natalie, Addison, Phoebe, and Kimberly, and Ellery, Nathan.

# ABOUT THE AUTHOR

Patti K. Owens is a lifelong letter writer. With her first book, she shares her experiences as a Stephen minister and a spiritual journalist through the many letters written over the years. She is an avid reader. She considers herself the ultimate optimist. She is a wife, mother, and grandmother, and finds great joy in all of those. She lives with her husband, Dan, in Lake Orion, Michigan, and looks forward to what each new day brings.

CPSIA information can be obtained
at www.ICGtesting.com
Printed in the USA
BVHW030444301221
624566BV00002B/9

9 781098 089986